VENTURI SCOTT BROWN & ASSOCIATES

ON HOUSES AND HOUSING

Architectural Monographs No 21

VENTURI SCOTT BROWN & ASSOCIATES
ON HOUSES AND HOUSING

A.D. ACADEMY EDITIONS / ST MARTIN'S PRESS

For Paul Davidoff, in memory

Architectural Monographs No 21
Editorial Offices
42 Leinster Gardens London W2 3AN

ISSN 0141-2191

Editorial and Design Team
Dr Andreas C Papadakis (Publisher)
Andrea Bettella (Senior Designer)
Vivian Constantinopoulos (House Editor)
James Steele (Contributing Editor)
Helen Castle, Lisa Kosky, Annamarie Uhr, Owen Thomas

Publisher's Note
I am deeply indebted to Robert Venturi and Denise Scott Brown for their permission to reproduce writings and original sketches. I would especially like to thank Denise Scott Brown for her close collaboration with myself, the editors and designers. Thanks also to the many members of Venturi, Scott Brown and Associates, for their research and for providing photographic material.   *ACP*

Cover: Coxe-Hayden House and Studio, Block Island, Rhode Island, photo by Tom Bernard; *P2*: Trubek House, Nantucket, Massachusetts, photo by Steven Izenour

First published in Great Britain in 1992 by
ACADEMY EDITIONS
An imprint of the Academy Group Ltd
42 Leinster Gardens London W2 3AN

ISBN 1 85490 0935 (HB)
ISBN 1 85490 0986 (PB)

Published in the United States of America in 1992 by
ST MARTIN'S PRESS
175 Fifth Avenue, New York, NY 10010

ISBN 0-312-07244-9 (HB)
ISBN 0-312-07148-5 (PB)

Printed and bound in Singapore

CONTENTS

Living the Legend in Philadelphia *James Steele*   6
On Houses and Housing *Denise Scott Brown*   10
The House as Microcosm and Macrocosm *James Steele*   14

PROJECTS AND WRITINGS

Beach House, Project, 1959   18
Foulkeways, Gwynedd, Project, 1959   20
Guild House, 1961   22
Vanna Venturi House, 1961   24
A Postscript on My Mother's House *Robert Venturi*, 1982
Vanna Venturi House Addition, Project, 1975   30
Meiss House, Project, 1962   31
Frug Houses I & II, Projects, 1965   32
Lieb House, 1967   34
Brighton Beach Housing Competition, 1967   36
Houses of Ill-Repute *Robert Venturi and Denise Scott Brown*, 1971   38
Hersey House, Project, 1968   39
D'Agostino House, Project, 1968   40
Wike House, Project, 1969   41
The Trubek and Wislocki Houses, 1970   42
House in Connecticut, 1970   44
Addition to the House in Connecticut, Project, 1976   48
Learning from Levittown, 1970   50
Remedial Housing for Architects Studio *Denise Scott Brown*, 1970;
Signs of Life: Symbols in the American City – The Home *Robert Venturi,
Steven Izenour and Denise Scott Brown*, 1976
Venturi House, Wissahickon Avenue, 1972 to Present   66
Wissahickon Avenue Housing, Project, 1972   68
Addition to House in Sea Isle City, 1972   70
Tucker House, 1974   71
Dream House, Project, 1974   74
House in Bermuda, 1975   75
House in Vail, 1975   78
Eclectic House, Project, 1977   82
House on Long Island I, Project, 1977   84
House in Absecon, Project, 1977   85
Princeton Housing, Project, 1978   86
House in Delaware, 1978   88
Chinatown Housing, 1979   92
'Mount Vernon' House, Project, 1979   94
Coxe-Hayden House and Studio, 1979   96
House on Nantucket Island, 1981   100
House on Long Island II, Project, 1981   101
House on Long Island III, 1982   102
Winterthur Housing, Project, 1983   104
House on Long Island IV, 1983   105

Changing Family Forms *Denise Scott Brown*, 1983   108
Housing Prototypes for Austin, Texas *Denise Scott Brown*, 1984   111
House at Stony Creek, 1984   114
Library for a House in Northern Italy, 1984   116
Sunshine Dream Village, Project, 1985   118
Pearl Houses, 1985   119
Memphis: A Housing Strategy *Denise Scott Brown*, 1984-89   122
House on Long Island V, 1985-90   130
House in Maine, 1986   134
House in Tuxedo Park, Project, 1987 to Present   140
Sketches for a House, 1990   141

Chronology of Houses and Housing Projects   142
Attributions with Photo Credits   144

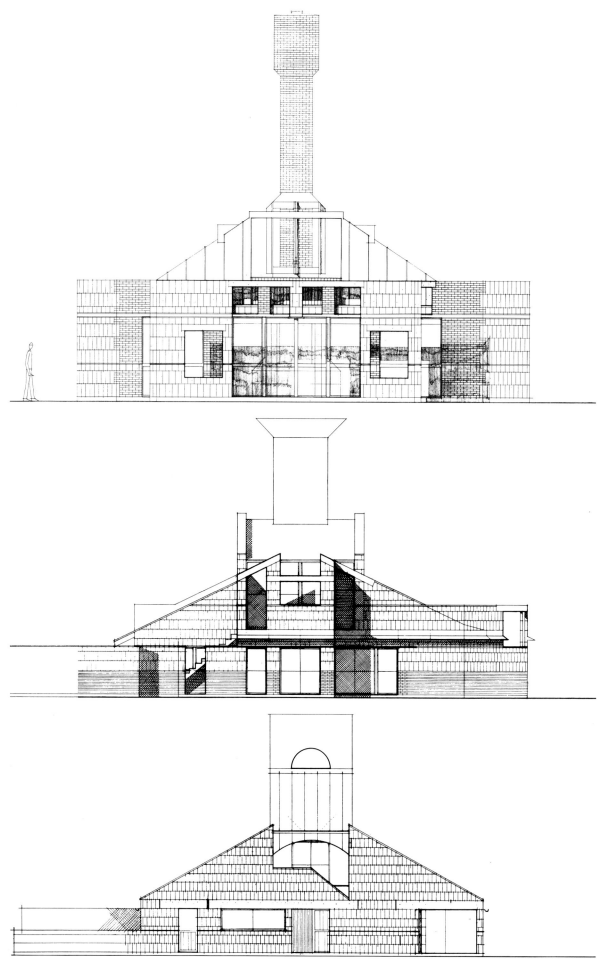

FROM ABOVE: VANNA VENTURI HOUSE, EARLY SCHEMES, 1962

LIVING THE LEGEND IN PHILADELPHIA

JAMES STEELE

While the history of the Philadelphia School still remains to be written, and many of its original members have either never reached an audience outside of their own region, or have changed direction entirely, Robert Venturi and Denise Scott Brown continue to personify and perpetuate the original spirit that began there. If the attentions of an increasingly fashion conscious profession and the public that followed it may now have focused on Los Angeles, New York and London, something far more substantial took place in Philadelphia during a period that roughly lasted from 1955 to 1974, with architectural repercussions that continue to surface in surprising and unexpected ways today. Just as Sci-Arc, or Cooper Union and the Architectural Association seem to attract specific groups at the moment, the University of Pennsylvania, under the leadership of Dean G Holmes Perkins, also began to be the focal point of a daunting array of talents at that time. Louis I Kahn was unquestionably the spiritual leader of the School, and others, such as Aldo Guirgola and Ian McHarg, had, and still continue to have, considerable influence, but the work that Robert Venturi was doing there in the early 60s unquestionably generated the most excitement among the students, and he developed a sizeable underground following. His book *Complexity and Contradiction in Architecture*, which was first released in 1966, had received an extensive preview in the Yale Journal *Perspecta* one year earlier, which was prophetically edited by Robert AM Stern, and the issue soon spread like wildfire through the studios.[1]

The book itself began as personal footnotes to a course in architectural theories that Venturi taught at Penn, with more than 350 small examples used like a series of lecture slides to incrementally establish an irrefutable thesis which has now been widely recognised as having totally changed the direction of architecture. Rather than simply being an attack on the Modern Movement, *Complexity and Contradiction* was, as it has been described, much more important as 'a civilised lesson in how to see'.[2] As a background to the achievements of Venturi and Scott Brown, it should be stated that for all of its progressive tendencies, the University of Pennsylvania, like every other Ivy League school of architecture at the time, was still completely Modernist in its outlook. While it may not have gone to the extreme of dropping history courses from the curriculum, as Walter Gropius did at Harvard, the credo manifested itself in other, equally effective ways. A talented student, for example, who was working part-time in the office of a local Vernacularist named Walter Durham, received a veiled warning at a preliminary jury for incorporating historical elements into his project, and when he persisted in doing so, was failed quite soundly. In spite of the revolutionaries within what Tom Wolfe has called 'the compound' the role models that were consistently put forward were Mies van der Rohe, Le Corbusier, and the other 'form-givers' of the Modern Movement. The integrity of what was considered to be culturally-redemptive internal space, and the honesty and clarity of the structure, circulation and light that defined it, as well as the legibility of the exterior form that contained it, was constantly and subliminally promoted in studio critiques, lectures and juries. In the process, we came to believe, with something close to parareligious zeal, that we had a mission to change the world through design. The very least we could do, until

the first client in need of redemption came along, was to paint our house or apartment white, buy as much uncomfortable architect-designed furniture as we could afford, and ignore the endless complaints about the psychological coldness and functional and environmental failures of Modern architecture that came from the great unwashed. Ada Louise Huxtable, who has played a central role as a commentator on this period, captured that attitude perfectly when she said: 'Architects sincerely believed that health and happiness were the natural corollaries of the right way of building; they even believed that human nature could be contained or changed by the right physical environment.'[3] In the transformation from the faith in growth and prosperity of the 50s to the disillusionment of the late 60s, it became clear that architecture, as well as literature, or art, or any other form of cultural expression for that matter, could not save the world, and that each of these disciplines would be fortunate enough to save themselves. The exact reasons for that transformation, and the social revolution that has accompanied it, have already been exhaustively analysed elsewhere, but the effect at the time was like an incremental shock treatment, in which assassinations were followed by riots; war and demonstrations; a seemingly endless nuclear nightmare; and one environmental disaster after another. The result was that science and technology, which had once held out the possibility of a better world, seemed to be defaulting on its promise, and it wasn't only the architectural credo that represented such promise that was on trial, but the ideals, morals and 'belief-systems' of society itself.[4] Enter 'the post-modern condition' and the absolute necessity of irony for psychic survival.

Venturi's 'Gentle Manifesto' also shared space with Louis Kahn's latest projects in that prescient 1965 issue of *Perspecta*, reflecting the symbiotic as well as competitive relationship that existed between them. In briefly comparing the two, it should first be noted that each had a firm basis in Modernist theory. As Robert Venturi himself has said: 'I have never intended to totally reject Modern architecture in words or work because I do, and I think our architecture should, in important ways, evolve out of it, not revolt against it. Its masterpieces hold their own with those of any age.'[5] But, what are those 'important ways'? For Kahn, the answer has much to do with buildings such as the Richards Medical Laboratory and the Dacca Assembly Hall, which are examples of a kind of historical abstraction that was considered to be acceptable by the Modernists. In this abstraction, specific monuments from the past were deemed suitable for inspiration, but not direct quotation, leading Kahn to include Scottish Castles, the towers of San Gimignano, and the Temples at Paestum among his sources. For Venturi and Scott Brown this kind of abstraction has also been consistently present, but because a more comprehensive, and virtually encyclopedic recollection of architectural history lies behind the selection of the references, they tend to be overlayed upon each other in ways that are frequently unintelligible to those who are less knowledgeable. In the Vanna Venturi house, which is one of the first instances of this kind of overlay, Michelangelo's Porta Pia, Le Corbusier's Villa Stein de Monzie at Garches, and Palladio's Villa Barbaro at Maser, as well as the fundamental, generic symbol for a Classical pediment are all present, just for a start. Such multiple references can be identified in virtually every design that the firm has produced, paradoxically becoming one of the 'important ways' that it relates to Modernism. In this regard, as Stanislaus von Moos has pointed out, Venturi's interest in historical architecture is primarily visual, and is 'motivated by a search for aesthetic principles . . . The authenticity that interests Venturi in buildings is thus not primarily social, historical or symbolic but rather the authenticity of their linkage to their respective environments, combined with which they constitute 'a perceptual whole'. To the extent to which Venturi thinks not as a historian but as a designer of urban spaces, he is an architect; to the extent that he allows himself to be guided by his eye – by subjective perception – he is part of a specifically modern tradition.'[6] The majority of the projects shown here illustrate the kind of linkage that Von Moos refers to.

Venturi and Kahn may have shared a penchant for historical abstraction to varying degrees, based on the differences in their awareness of sources, but they most certainly parted company over a strong emphasis on structuralism which was promoted by Kommendant, as well as on the concepts of 'existence will' and 'served' and 'servant' spaces which were simply further refinements of functionalism. While *Complexity and Contradiction* may have shocked purists who still believed that less was more, its historicism was still understandable – and acceptable. With the publication of *Learning from Las Vegas* in 1972, however, a definite schism was opened. Aside from the obvious heresy of proposing that such a crassly commercial example as Las Vegas could help teach architects how to synthesise irrefutable aspects of the built environment and to communicate them more effectively to others, the final formalisation of the ideas of the 'duck' and 'the decorated shed' make this book equally significant. Kahn's 'wrapping ruins' around the unbuilt meeting place of the Salk Institute and the exterior zone of the Dacca Assembly, which many feel had been inspired by Venturi's first use of layering at the North Penn Visiting Nurse Association Building in Ambler in 1961, show a flirtation with the separation of form and function, but fall far short of the divorce represented by *Learning from Las Vegas*.[7]

Socio-Plastics and Social Relevance

Robert Venturi's collaboration with Denise Scott Brown, which had started in 1964, began to add an entirely new and much more humanistic dimension to the firm. In this expansion, in which the 'visual aesthetic' and reliance on literary discourse described by Von Moos were balanced with social consciousness, a more inclusive and wide-ranging agenda of concerns has emerged.

Denise Scott Brown entered the Architectural Association as a fourth year student in 1952, and soon became interested in the work of Alison and Peter Smithson, who were part of the Independent Group at the Institute of Contemporary Art. She, with a small number of students from the AA, sought them out before they became well known in the profession, and their ideas had a lasting influence on her. 'As I understood the Smithson phrase "active socio-plastics,"' she has said, 'it meant that architects should design for the real life of the street and for the way communities actually work, even if the results are not conventionally pleasing. There was, I think, an unspoken desire to derive, from a community life that was not immediately beautiful, a deeper beauty, and an intention not to abandon architecture but to make it socially relevant.'[8] Following this, she went to the University of Pennsylvania in 1958, where she was taught by the urban sociologist Herbert Gans who reinforced the Smithsons' idea that processes and patterns could be discovered and built upon if approached with an open mind.

Finding and expressing those patterns, as well as the significance behind social norms, has been one of the main goals of the firm since she has become involved with it and that determination is certainly evident in *Learning from Las Vegas*, which is unequivocal in its expression of support for variety over uniformity. For evidence of this view, it is only necessary to read the 'Theory of Ugly and Ordinary and Related and Contrary Theories', which presents one of the clearest and most perceptive criticisms of the Modern Movement that has been written. Two decades after its first appearance this analysis has lost none of its polemic pertinence. As a plea to architects to look at the world as 'what it is' rather than 'what it ought to be', the 'Theory of Ugly and Ordinary' is the equivalent of the statement of disbelief in the fairy tale about the Emperor's new clothes, in which the child sees what others preferred to pretend did not exist. Whilst representing a natural extension of the ideas first put forward in *Complexity and Contradiction*, *Learning From Las Vegas* presents them in a more empirical, and less historically referential way. In expanding upon the innovative work by Donald Appleyard, Kevin Lynch and John Myer in *A View From the Road*, for example, Venturi, Scott Brown and Izenour have added a qualitative dimension to this underestimated but important field of study, and confirm a reality that has yet to be acknowledged by architects today.

While only obliquely related to houses and housing, two examples from personal experience may serve to show how these ideas have been successfully implemented. Jim Thorpe, as the first of these, is a small town in upstate Pennsylvania that has suffered the same economic hardships as others in the coal region around it following the closing of the mines here in the mid-1950s, but unlike them it has had the advantage of beautiful natural surroundings and a location that has protected it from change. A visit to the town today is like a trip into a time warp, since a majority of the buildings along the main street, which date from the turn of the century, have survived intact. In 1979, VSBA were asked by the Carbon County Planning Commission to assist in trying to achieve a more lasting revival, and the firm chose to focus on what they have called 'the interaction of the image, associations and atmosphere of this heritage with new uses and activities that restore economic viability and renewed purpose in the present'[9]. Through a series of subtle, but extremely effective tactics such as conversion and restoration, signage, lighting, paving, street furniture and store-front improvements, as well as the provision of more parking in unobtrusive, yet conveniently located parts of town, Jim Thorpe has now found new life and is crowded with visitors each weekend.

Franklin Court, which is more formally known as the Benjamin Franklin Memorial Park, is another successful example of sensitive intervention into an equally delicate urban context. When asked by the Federal Park Service to restore both the printing shop and the house of this famous Philadelphian, the architects were concerned about the fact that nothing except the foundations of the original structure had survived, which would have meant a speculative restoration at best. Since both buildings were built according to instructions that Franklin had sent in numerous letters to his wife while he was the American Ambassador to France, however, detailed descriptions of vital dimensions, such as the number of storeys and fireplaces in the house, did exist. These descriptions prompted a counter proposal that the house be ghosted out in steel frame to give a sense of its presence rather than a problematic physical representation which could not be authenticated. In addition, the architects proposed an underground museum as an alternative to the one they had been asked to provide at ground level. This solution not only retained the original setting described by Franklin, but also gave the open frames additional impact because of the elimination of visual clutter. The entrance to the underground museum, which may have presented an insurmountable problem to a designer with less skill, is now incorporated in a long arcade that runs along a recess in the garden wall, becoming a perfectly believable continuation of the partially real and partially fantastic setting that has been created here. Seen through a long passageway that connects Market Street with this interior courtyard, and which passes under the conventionally restored Post Office that Franklin had established there, the open steel frames have an eerie quality to them, and are actually far more memorable than an inaccurate reproduction because they allow visitors to fill in the details of the houses in their own imagination, based on the clues that the architects present. By resisting the considerable temptation to simply follow the original brief, which would have resulted in just one more pristine, but historically dubious restoration of the kind that has become typical of this part of Philadelphia, Venturi and Scott Brown have managed to provide a much more appropriate memorial to a remarkable man.

Ironically, while the record of examples of the firm's ingenuity goes on, the actual project list of the office is limited in comparison to other firms of such high stature, because the chance to actually utilise such valuable insights has been given to others, rather than the architects that developed them. They themselves say that:

> Most of the complexities and contradictions we relished thinking about we did not use, because we did not have the opportunity.[10]

In the final acknowledgement of the contribution that they have made to the diverse architectural scene today, the circumstances behind that long exclusion, as well as the rancour that surrounded it, have now been all but forgotten, which provides a poignant reminder of the selective public memory that has become symptomatic of the Information Age. In the relatively short period of time since *Complexity and Contradiction* and *Learning from Las Vegas* were written, a social cycle, at least in the Western World, has been completed and the syndrome that Martin Pawley has identified as 'information anxiety' has now become endemic. As a consequence of too much information and too little time to absorb it, this condition has not only been accompanied by collective amnesia, but also by a baffling proliferation of literary allusions that go far beyond the original intention of VSBA to use words in order to prompt linguistic associations with architecture. As a consequence, words have become an indispensable aegis of authority for all aspiring architects and books have become shields to hide behind rather than sources of fresh ideas. Where it may once have been necessary to do professional battle in order to establish the fact that architecture, like language, has semiological components that can be effectively utilised to send signals to those experiencing it, words are now seen as being integral with, rather than analogous to, built reality. Architecture is no longer considered to be like a text, but has become the text itself, and as a result, each new movement is considered to be illegitimate without a titular sage to give it literary credibility.

Machiavelli in Academia

The tendency towards exclusivity, which has plagued the profession since architects began to think of themselves as individual creative agents, now seems to have been magnified. While describing archaeology, John Baines could just as well have been talking about architecture when he said that: 'Any discipline is nearly closed and tends to seek closure, requiring both that a particular body of material and methods be learned and that formal qualifications or "initiation" be acquired, often with elaborate rituals.'[11] That tendency towards closure is particularly evident in the majority of literary references used today, and while once confined to writers and poets such as Kenneth Burke, TS Eliot and Cleanth Brooks, the current explosion of the concept that tectonics is the equivalent of text has now taken an architecture of signs into an entirely new, and considerably more arcane realm. As critic Sylvia Lavin has said: 'Theory in architecture is clearly a mixed blessing today. Having been central to the profession's ability to move beyond the sterility of Late-Modernism by way of Robert Venturi's *Complexity and Contradiction*, it has since become equally central to . . . a Machiavellian labyrinth.'[12] The double-edged literary sword that Venturi introduced so effectively in that book has even now been used to attack its basic premise, with the subjugation of the word 'contradiction' itself to Derridian Deconstruction, in order to expose its 'Hegelian ancestry'.[13] All of this shows that in today's hypermedia climate, nothing is sacred and that words, like statistics, can be used to prove anything.

As an alternative, Venturi, in both 'Diversity, Relevance and Representation in Historicism, or *Plus ça change*', delivered in 1982, and a joint presentation with Denise Scott Brown called 'Architecture as Shelter, City as Decon' given this year, has repetitively made a 'Plea for Pattern All Over'. Instead of the irrelevant 'Parvenu Classicism' that he criticised in the first article, or the 'Architecture as Frozen Theory' approach that was identified as having replaced fundamentals in the second, both Venturi and Scott Brown have recommended a return to basics, and an objective reassessment of the proper potential of ornament.

In this espousal of 'all-over pattern', there is a tacit understanding that architects today rarely have the opportunity to choose the context around the buildings they design, and must cope with the realities of asphalt and freeways as well as the occasional high bluff overlooking the ocean in Bermuda. If style, as Louis Sullivan once said, is totally defined by response to surroundings, then the style of these architects continues to be appropriate.

Notes

1 *Perspecta 9/10: The Yale Architectural Journal*, Robert AM Stern, Ed, New Haven, Connecticut, 1965, pp 18-56.
2 Ada Louise Huxtable, 'Is Modern Architecture Dead?', *The New York Review of Books*, New York, 1981.
3 *Ibid*.
4 *Ibid*.
5 Robert Venturi, 'Diversity, Relevance and Representation in Historicism, or *Plus ça change* . . . plus a Plea for Pattern all over Architecture with a Postscript on my Mother's House', in *A View from the Campidoglio*, Robert Venturi and Denise Scott Brown, Icon Editions, Harper Row, New York, 1984, p 115.
6 Stanislaus von Moos, *Venturi, Rauch and Scott Brown Buildings and Projects*, Rizzoli International, New York, 1987, pp 13-14.
7 Robert Venturi, Denise Scott Brown and Steven Izenour, *Learning from Las Vegas*, MIT Press, Cambridge, Mass, 1972, p xviii.
8 Denise Scott Brown, 'Urban Concepts', *Architectural Design* 60:1-2: 90, p 31.
9 *Ibid*, p 54.
10 Robert Venturi, Denise Scott Brown and Steven Izenour, *op cit*, p 129.
11 John Baines, 'Restricted Knowledge, Hierarchy and Decorum: Modern Perceptions and Ancient Institutions', *Journal of the American Research Centre in Egypt*, Vol XXVII, 1990, Cairo, p 5.
12 Sylvia Lavin, 'The Uses and Abuses of Theory', *Progressive Architecture* 08: 90, p 114.
13 G Bennington, 'Complexity without Contradiction in Architecture', *AA Files*, Annals of the Architectural Association School of Architecture, No 14, 1987, p 15.

ON HOUSES AND HOUSING

DENISE SCOTT BROWN

There was a time, not long ago, when many architects, perhaps most young architects, wanted to be housers. Architects of the Modern Movement saw social housing and architecture as virtually coterminous. Their plans for a brave new world figured mainly housing. Other components of urban life, while considered, were defined with much less emotional intensity than was the housing. Architects whose biggest commission was a small house, dreamed of cities for millions. The individual house was deemed an unworthy design task, unless it was treated as a point of departure or prototype for mass housing. Industrialisation of housing construction was to be the means of solving the housing problem – Le Corbusier's statement, 'architecture or revolution', referred to this ideal. In addition, housing was to be high-rise and light-seeking; on-the-ground, single-family, detached, suburban housing was scorned.

Today, architects' ideals about housing are as flat as the housing market. Two decades of reduced funding for social housing have contributed to this situation, as has the tendency of the times to turn away from social problems; yet the theories and ideals of the Modern Movement have also made it harder for architects to become involved in the real problems of housing.

Over the last 30 years, events and colleagues (for example the social planners), have pushed architects to rethink the housing ideals of early Modern architecture. This has been a slow process involving many stages. My first experience of this questioning was in William Wheaton's course on housing at the University of Pennsylvania. With Roehampton, Greenlane and Ville Radieuse in my mind, I was launched into the social economy of American housing. I learned the structure of the housing industry (atomistic, decentralised) and of the housing market (regional) and heard why mass-produced, prefabricated housing was no panacea; I discovered that what looked like social housing in Europe, was, in America, housing for the rich, which had in fact driven the poor into denser slums; I discovered that, in England and America, public housing does not house the poorest, most needy of the population and that the welter of housing programmes, whose acronym names Americans called 'alphabet soup', cover a scandalously small portion of the housing need.

Herbert Gans taught that one set of social values, honourable though they may be, should not prevail over all other sets. Why should there be only one theme in housing for a large city? Was Levittown necessarily wrong? Regional economists and transportation engineers pointed out that, with suburbanisation, the journey to work could become shorter rather than longer, because work places decentralised too, and that the emerging suburban pattern was not necessarily a detrimental one.

At Penn, the problem of housing in developing areas was viewed as one of evolving an economy that would allow self-help methods to work, as a partnership between families and government. These complex arrangements for getting housing built, using multiple sources of funds and several types of labour, seemed to me to be not too different from the situation for acquiring housing in developed areas, where a mixture of economic mechanisms and the contribution of the individual owner provide an equally complex package.

Remedial Housing for Architects

In our academic and professional lives since the early 1960s, we have developed our own questions and issues in housing that have amounted to a self-re-education on the topic.

Like most young architects, our first commissions were to design quite small houses for close relatives and, what we called, 'tea and sympathy' clients; yet at the same time we were taking a broad view of housing, as academics and urban planners.

Immersed in both experiences, we began to question the lack of societal worth of the individual house. Our house clients were teaching us a great deal about the relation of their lives to buildings. A young poet, commissioning a small house in the woods, sent us a poem, 'Portrait of the House As Myself'. 'The house' he said, 'is shy but eloquent.' Our second thoughts on Modern architects' distaste for the single house appear in the article, 'Some Houses of Ill-Repute'.

We continued to work in housing where we could, for the clients that chose us. This meant designing small houses for individuals and, when the opportunity presented itself, in our role as planners specifying housing programmes for low-income families. We were able to design assisted housing for the elderly in Guild House and for moderate income families in Chinatown in Philadelphia. In these projects we designed for people we could not meet as private clients, but had to understand through committees that represented them. We also had to achieve sturdiness with modest budgets. Another project, Brighton Beach Competition, helped us verbalise our philosophy of 'ugly and ordinary' – because this was what Philip Johnson called our entry at the jury.

In 1970, we continued our broader study of housing through a studio at Yale called 'Remedial Housing for Architects or Learning from Levittown'. Here we furthered the analysis of symbolism initiated in our Las Vegas studio, taking our investigation into the environment of the house. We attempted to describe different values on housing, including our own, setting them within the broad context of American taste cultures. We were, in a sense, producing the architectural counterpart to Gans' Levittown study and his later analyses of taste cultures.[1] The programmes from this studio are included in this book, with those of our findings that were part of our 'Signs of Life: Symbols in the City' exhibition at the Smithsonian Institution in 1976. While the exhibition staked out the territory of symbolism in the home, the subject of the studio was broader; 'Remedial Housing for Architects' was an attempt to redefine what should be the totality of architects' concerns with the architectural aspects of housing.

Architecture and the Social Economy of Housing

Why can't American architects get to do housing, we asked? This question devolved into several others. First, why can't we design housing for low-income people? The answer was not only, as in our case, because no one asked us; it was also that so little of this housing is built. Therefore dedicated architects who aim to produce the maximum housing possible for the poor find they must step back from design and concentrate, rather, on implementation. Here architects become economic strategists and social activists, seeking funding mechanisms, partnerships between private and public, or any tactic available at the time. These architects' actions parallel those of architects in developing areas who abandon the design and production of individual houses in favour of providing sites and urban infrastructure and allowing people (with minimal financial and construction help) to build their own houses. The techniques evolved by activist groups and squatters – perhaps particularly those that solved the housing problem in Karachi[2] – may have relevance for the intractable housing problems of urban America, not in their illegality, but in their realistic yet imaginative organisation techniques.

Getting students to think realistically rather than ideologically about social housing is part of the remedial housing project: helping them understand that poor and semi-poor people need old housing, and that not all areas of the city should be renewed beyond the point where people with low income can afford them. In the best of worlds this shouldn't be necessary; in our world it's better than no housing. Even more agonised reasoning must be applied to the problem of the homeless. Whether our society could or should approach this problem at the scale that it requires is not a question; but immediately, a way is needed to help homeless people make the best of what they have, where they are.

The second aspect of the question was why can't architects design housing for the middle classes – for the Levittowns, or their equivalents today? The answer is again partly that not much of this housing is being built. Where it is built, it is produced, in the main, by small-scale merchant builders who do not feel they have need of architects to sell to their particular customers. There is room, to some extent, for architects in upper-middle income urban housing and in housing for the rich. But methods of financing and producing most housing in America don't call for architects, and most people don't miss them. If the scale of production became much greater, architects could be involved in the design of prototypes, and architects with a realistic understanding of housing *could* have a role in improving the industry's ability to meet America's housing need. But in the area where mass production has achieved its greatest success, in trailer housing and mobile homes, architects have played an unimportant part, and where industrial techniques have been used in the building industry – in the mass production of traditional housing components or the vertical integration of building trades – architects haven't noticed it.

Architects who decry the pre-industrial nature of housing construction might not be happy with the increases in social and economic scale that would be required to produce the centralised housing industry of their dreams. This goes for mega-structures too. Even if we discount the paucity of vision that suggests that all pods in a mega-structure would be the same, the whole doesn't work in other respects. How does the pod grow to allow grandmother to live with the family? If space is left for grandmother's future pod, the relation of numbers of pods to amount of infrastructure provided will not be an economical one. If space is not left, the only way to change is to move to another mega-structure. A mega-structure implies an enormous change in lifestyle once, and then no further changes.

My ideal for housing is not the mega-structure, but it isn't Seaside either. Seaside is a beautiful town and a worthy effort but it can't serve as a substitute for a housing policy. Architects need to realise that many forms of housing should be available in a large, complex city. A regional housing strategy should allow for an array of housing opportunities: high-rise housing, Levittowns, Seasides, garden apartments, all manner of town-housing, old houses, public housing, and housing for all income groups and many different demographic categories and family types.[3] Many forms of relationship to town and country should be available, including an occasional mega-structure, and even the houses of architects. A citizen-activist, outraged by a strident architectural *oeuvre*, once suggested that cities should have an 'RR' zoning category: 'radical

residential, where you could put all the houses designed by radical architects. Let them enjoy each other.'

I am personally more interested in considering housing in the regional economy and housing symbolism in the cultural landscape than I am in trying to design a better prefab house, urban megastructure, or upper-income suburb. But the elemental house, the house the child draws, the house in the toy-train town, has great allure. Finding that archetype – not necessarily the same one for all regions – is an attractive challenge, like the challenge Le Corbusier set himself in the Domino Houses. And, at the other end of the scale, evolving a taxonomy for all Amerian housing – for houses and housing, private and public, from 'RR' to Levittown to the urban rowhouse – and considering this housing in the physical, cultural, socio-economic, technical and organisational contexts in which it evolved, were the ambitious aims of the Learning from Levittown Studio; aims needed, we felt, to help define roles for architects in housing today.

We told the students that architects should play different roles based on the housing type they are designing and on their own position in the structure of decision-making. Approaches to the design of housing and of houses should not be the same. When the architect knows the client only through a committee or statistics, a different way of designing is called for from that employed when considering the needs of an individual family one meets and talks with. However, future generations' claims on the individually-designed house should be kept in mind, and discussed with the client, and each unit of housing should be designed as a home.

Urban Houses

Here is a set of questions on urban housing I asked a beginning class of architecture students in 1962:

'The House' and 'Home'

What is this 'cell'? What does all city housing share in common that can be expressed by the concept of 'the house'? If 'home' is an abstract quality that a family gives to 'a house' and that depends on many conditions outside the physical structure itself, to the extent that the physical structure has power to do so, what makes a cell feel like a 'home'? What makes it resemble an open shelf or slot for the storage of people and goods? What is the meaning of the term 'identity'? What is the relation between the identity of the cell and the identity of the whole of which it forms part?

Privacy

What is its nature in the city? What kind of privacy do we need where? What is the problem of overlooking and eavesdropping? If total privacy is impossible in the city, will we be satisfied in some places with the illusion of privacy? In the city garden how do we maintain this illusion?

Sociability

To the extent that physical form can affect social patterns, can we plan our housing to allow people to make social patterns and contacts of their own choosing? Are closed cul de sacs 'more friendly'? Or do they enforce a type of 'hot house gregariousness'? Is there a 'way out' for deviants? Are apartment blocks socially isolated? In Sheffield? If the layout of the kraal and associated huts strongly reflects the African family and social pattern, to what extent, especially in the notions of privacy and sociability, do they compare with ours?

Public, Private and Semi-private

The Mapoch village, the houses on St Mark's Square (West Philadelphia), Pei's townhouses – each presents a public face and a private face. Pei's is proud and reticent, in the townhouse tradition; in West Philadelphia the culture of porch and rocking chair makes a pleasant semi-private lining to the public street, much augmenting the possibilities for an architecture of the street. In the Mapoch village most of life takes place on the sun-baked mud terraces of many levels that run beside the courtyard walls of the houses and serve as vantage point for viewing spectacles and the spectacle of life. Behind the facades, in each case, the spaces range from public to private, from formal to informal, from extrovert to introvert. From urban to rural?

The Private and the 'Faceless' Client. The Development House
It is possible to plan 'a house' for known clients, though even then artistic and economic reasons suggest that the needs of 'the house' be met too. With the house for an unknown client, whose wants are expressed statistically as an average or aggregation of individuals' wants, the architect must consider an apparent paradox: the house must be neutral enough to allow these unknown people to impress their own needs and expressions upon it; yet its forms must be evocative enough to challenge them to do so, and to provide a good base for the accretion and nurturing of a thousand private symbols. More than 90 percent of housing is built by tract builders, usually without help of architects. Can the architect afford to be in this position?

Houses that can Change
Most housing in medieval towns is medieval only in its basic structure; its internal components have seen many changes over the centuries or they would be unusable today. Large portions of West Philadelphia have accommodated gracefully to the change from single-family to apartment and rooming houses, and seen their ground floors converted to shops. Can we think of today's housing as being composed of a permanent supporting structure and short-lived infilling made of standardised industrial components easily removed and replaced? Isn't this better than the social disruption involved in the concept of the Kleenex City?

Industrialisation
Sooner or later this must hit the building industry. The home building industry is, in fact, nearest to it (cf Levitt's operation). America needs to build almost one million more houses per year than she is building if she is to catch up with her backlog within 30 years and provide housing conditions which she feels are fitting for the majority of her population. The architect's role in the handling of this emergency has been almost nil. He has not joined with those who set up the means and laws for quick, cheap house building, and now he contemplates the results of their actions (the Levittowns) with horror. Yet it is partly his fault. He has refused, in this way, to assume his ancient role of adviser to the king (today the public agency and the bureaucracy). Even in his other role as maker of taste he has lagged far behind his 18th-century counterpart, and has only the 'split-level rancher' to offer as his contribution (much distorted) to the domestic taste of the age. He is much needed today in the devising of modular systems of components (and of philosophies for their putting together) in an industrialised system of home and city building.

The Architecture of the Street: Provisions for the Automobile
What is the nature of the street which serves a small group of 'cells'? What can we learn from the Marseilles Unité, Elfreth's Alley, the Certosa di Pavia, St Mark's Square (West Philadelphia), Sheffield, Lasdun's Cluster Blocks, the Vicar's Close at Wells Cathedral? To what extent can a small street serving a few cells resemble an access balcony in a block of apartments? If it were no longer and gave equivalent weather protection, would city dwellers be prepared to park their cars and walk along it to their front doors? Should the car sit, so to speak, on the front porch? What of the guest's car? Can we solve the problem of parking, entry and

intelligibility better than was done at Radburn? Finally car and man must come together. From what point should they be separated?

The Cell
What conditions its overall width and length?
Orientation: What kind of light is best for a bedroom, kitchen, study, living-room, bathroom? To what extent need orientation be affected by the exigencies of climate?
Aspect: What kind of a 'view' will do? of a street? a walled garden? city roof? Must one see the sky? a tree? What should one see from the kitchen window? the bedroom and living-room windows?
Light: Given normal ceiling heights (approximately nine feet), light from a single source at the end of a room will not penetrate further than about 17 feet. What solutions have been found historically and today to the problem of lighting the centres of cell houses? Compare an 18th-century townhouse solution with a modern 'open plan' one.
Sizes: How has the problem of the narrow unit been faced historically and today? How did Georgian houses achieve a semblance of breadth and elegance in their public spaces? Does the Modern architect's use of the dropped living room and the dining space which is raised but part of the same space achieve a similar elegance? How does this pattern affect or reflect today's living patterns?
Circulation: How can the 'architecture of movement' within the building be made to seem shorter and less constricted than it necessarily is in a rowhouse?
Services: In a many-celled structure, services (all forms – including circulation) become a bulky part of the total structure. Small diseconomies get multiplied by the many units into great wastes. How can services be planned to be an economical and unobtrusive yet flexible and reachable part of the total structure?

Scale
We have talked of sizes and shapes and of the need for illusion in the creation of a sense of space and feeling of elegance (should 'the house' be 'elegant' or 'domestic'? or either or both?). How does the problem of scale enter into this? How does the scale of the single unit relate to the scale of the whole and to the city? In the Royal Crescent at Bath? In Ronald Turner's new housing on Osage and 45th Streets (W Philadelphia)? In the affluent Victorian rowhouses around 4009 Pine Street? At the Vicar's Close at Wells? At the Certosa di Pavia? Has this anything to do with the questions of 'identity' with which we started?[4]

Most of that I would stand by now (except for the use, here and in other reprinted articles in this volume, of the pronoun 'he' for the architect). Since that time we have had the opportunity to design a number of private houses but sadly little townhousing or social housing.

House as Odyssey
If the design of single-family houses is a self-indulgent activity with little redeeming social value, it is also a means for young architects to start their practice and learn their craft. For Bob Venturi, the design of single houses is a personal adventure and a method of wrestling with ideas that beset him at other scales on larger projects. During the years when he was designing his mother's house, he taught himself the basics of architecture by tackling the problem of the house over and over again. The Vanna Venturi house has been a point of departure for most of our other houses. Even our most recent houses take off, in many ways, from its basic *parti*. These are also the areas where Bob is most personally and individually involved. I am less part of the design of the houses than of any other aspect of our office's work. But Bob has collaborated on them with such members of our firm as Arthur

Jones, Frederic Schwartz, John Chase, Perry Kulper, Fran Read, and Steven Wiesenthal.

The unbuilt Beach House started the journey. Its tall chimney was a leave-taking, too, from the canons of Modern architecture, particularly from the International Style but also from the low-slung chimney-walls of Frank Lloyd Wright's houses. However, the Vanna Venturi house was Bob's main training vehicle. Over perhaps five years he designed seven versions of this house, making his first statement on everything that has been important to him in architecture since. He has, over the last 25 years, interpreted and reinterpreted this house for himself, based on questions of the time, seeing it as Mannerist, Classicist, a child's house, an old lady's house, a Chestnut Hill house, an apartment on the ground, a *jeu d'esprit*, an elemental shelter and many other things. Most recently he has seen it as an elemental house – a return to the archetype. Looking back on this house in the context of the heroic and original late Modernism of the 60s – including that of Louis Kahn – we realise its most significant characteristic might be that it looks like a house. It is not original, not heroic but rather, conventional and ordinary, in its specific, not implicit, references. In not being revolutionary it is astonishingly revolutionary.

My interpretations of it are urbanistic. In one sense it is a suburban house that has borrowed a vocabulary from the old suburb in which it sits, recessive on its lot, surrounded by lawn and trees whose colour it apes. But as much as any townhouse, this house has a proudly reticent urban front and a light-seeking, less formal back. If American houses are Queen Anne in front and Mary Anne behind, this one is Palladio in front and Aalto at the back. Yet its frontal formality is broken in many ways – literally by the broken pediment, which suggests an inside more convoluted than the outside, and by the use of simple minded, child-like windows, not quite formally composed; the simple-mindedness masks the complexity of a whole whose composition is modelled on Michelangelo's Porta Pia.

Inside, beyond the Lutyensesque broken axis, the house owes most to the Le Corbusier of the Villa Savoye, in its combinations of curves and planes and its tight conflation of sub-spaces to make one tautly-held main space. The 'nowhere stair' that runs behind the large fireplace is Furness with De Chirico out of Colonial America. It is also childhood's attic stair. It turns the residual space between fireplace and facade into an aggressively present object. Background becomes foreground in this ironic game. If every architect puts a chapel somewhere in every building, this entrance-staircase-fireplace is the chapel of this building.

Symbolically the house meditates upon all the archetypal, Anglo-Saxon images of house – the roof, the chimney, the symmetrical (more-or-less) windows and centrally placed front door – yet it juxtaposes these with broader quotations on architectural history, the Modern Movement, and latter-day American suburban Palladianism. This concatenation of themes has been our range ever since. The house itself has become an icon; we see it on top of hospital buildings, apartment houses, and corporate office towers. In our own work, its themes suffer a sea change, primarily in relation to environment. It becomes 'a straight arrow' in the woods, a battered arrow in snow country; its Palladianism assumes an industrial tinge and a green colour for a family of art collectors in Connecticut, and a looser-limbed, stucco picturesqueness, culled from the *genius loci*, for the same family in Bermuda.

If the Beach House was the first Shingle Style Revival house of Post-Modernism, some later houses have carried this theme further on the beach in Nantucket or Block Island and in the snow mountains in Vail. Others have been conditioned by wind-swept locations and views of the ocean. All have toyed with the relation between public and private and the gradation from one to the other as the house is penetrated. In this time of Decon, the elemental sheltering quality of the roof has become important to us and we are intrigued by the idea of the simple, walled, eaved shelter that contains within it a complexity of wooden architecture protected from the rain. In this, the temple architecture of the Far East is meaningful to us; it has led us to reinterpret the Vanna Venturi house as shelter with a taut skin wound around it and a complex life within it.[5]

Does a house that combines Palladio, Aalto, Lutyens, Le Corbusier, Mary Anne and the Porta Pia bear too much architectural and symbolic freight? Indubitably, it's overdone. The house is like a puppy with large feet. But it *is* an architect's house, used almost as a lab. Our own house served this function at a later time. We did not gut its interior to create Piranesi-Modern space, but refurnished it and stencilled its walls in an exaggerated way that taught us about ornament and pattern, and fired our enthusiasm for decorative arts and artistic sources from the early 20th century.

And although the Vanna Venturi house is usually described in stylistic and formal terms, functional requirements were not ignored in its planning, they were merely not discussed in our writing. The house works in the narrowly functional sense but, it satisfies, as well, a broader range of functions. For example, it was intended for a widow and perhaps her companion, and was designed specifically around her antique and reproduction furniture. It was located to give her accessibility to transportation and urban services yet to provide privacy as well. Being no larger than a generous apartment, it has adapted easily to the needs of its new owners, an empty-nest family. It can suit a two-person working family, newly-weds, or a family with one child. For a while, Bob and I lived in the upstairs room. It was like waking up under a tent. This room is now the study of the academic who owns it.

The house provided Vanna with company and solace when she was an old woman, living there with an architecture student on the second floor for protection. Carloads, sometimes busloads, of visitors, mainly architecture students, would come by, and we would find her with a seminar seated around the dining table giving lectures on the architecture of the house and babyhood of its architect. The house filled some long hours for her. As her son put it, 'Architecture is the opiate of the mothers.'

Notes

1 Herbert J Gans, *The Levittowners: Ways of Life and Politics in a New Suburban Community*, Columbia University Press, New York, 1967; and *Popular Culture and High Culture: an Analysis and Evaluation of Taste*, Basic Books, New York, 1974. See also Denise Scott Brown, 'Architectural Taste in a Pluralistic Society', *The Harvard Architectural Review*, Vol 1, Spring 1980, pp 41-51.
2 Arif Hasan, 'The Housing Programme of the Orangi Pilot Project', *Initiatives in Grassroots Participation*, workshop organised by the Pakistan Administrative Staff College, Lahore, and the United Nations Co-ordinators Groups for South Asia, Karachi, December 7-9, 1985, and 'The Low Cost Sanitation Programme' of the Orangi Pilot Project, Karachi, Pakistan, *Workshop on Community Health and the Urban Poor*, organised by OXFAM and the London School of Hygiene and Tropical Medicine, Oxford, July 7-12, 1985.
3 Denise Scott Brown, 'Changing Family Forms', below.
4 Denise Scott Brown, 'Housing in the City', unpublished course material for Architecture 411, Fall 1962, Graduate School of Fine Arts, University of Pennsylvania.
5 See Robert Venturi and Denise Scott Brown, 'Two Naifs in Japan', in *Architecture and Decorative Arts,* catalogue of an exhibition of work by Venturi Scott Brown and Associates, Knoll International, Japan, and Kajima Press, Tokyo, 1991.

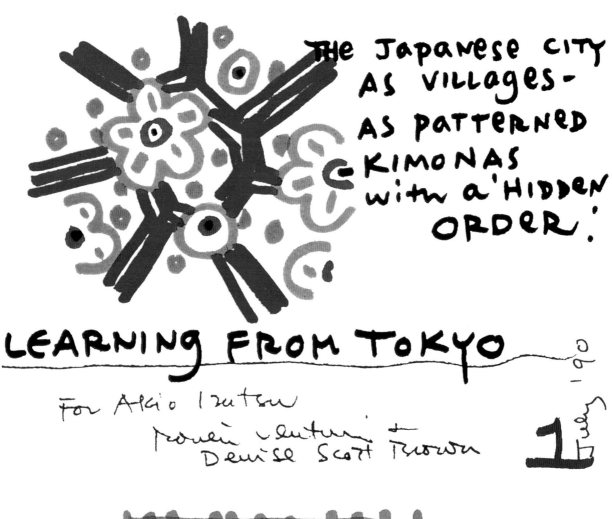

THE JAPANESE CITY AS VILLAGES— AS PATTERNED KIMONAS with a 'HIDDEN ORDER!

LEARNING FROM TOKYO

For Akio Izutsu

Robert Venturi & Denise Scott Brown

1 July '90

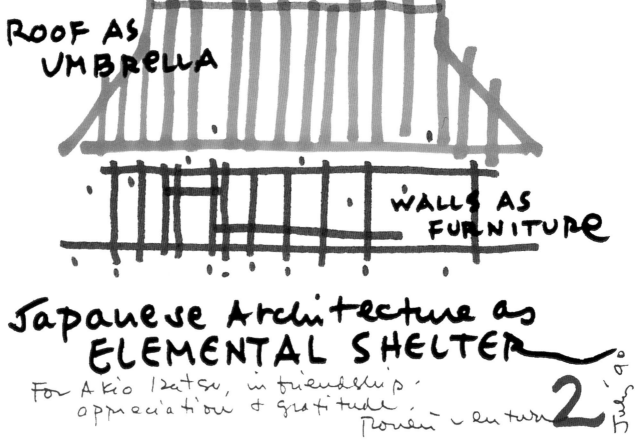

ROOF AS UMBRELLA

WALLS AS FURNITURE

Japanese Architecture as ELEMENTAL SHELTER

For Akio Izutsu, in friendship, appreciation & gratitude. Robert Venturi

2 July '90

ABOVE AND BELOW: CONCEPTUAL SKETCHES FOR JAPANESE ARCHITECTURE, 1990

THE HOUSE AS MICROCOSM AND MACROCOSM

JAMES STEELE

If there is any truth to the aphorism that a house presents an architect with a microcosm of all of the design issues that will ever be faced elsewhere, then Robert Venturi has explored that world more thoroughly than most. Yet, he and Denise Scott Brown have, in design and research, also taken the subject of architects' housing out of the arcane world of Modern architectural ideology and into Levittown, remaking a relationship from individual houses to housing and from the unique and elite to the general and the popular. There is a remarkable consistency in this oeuvre over the last three decades, from the first Beach House of 1959 to the most recent houses on Long Island, finished in 1990, indicating the intentional reconstruction of similar themes that are seen to require restatement.

Two of the most prevalent of these themes, which have been acknowledged by the architects themselves, and are both present in varying degrees in each of their houses, are Romanticism and the Classical Renaissance. As the historical antithesis of rationality, Romanticism has always implied an emotional, rather than a purely analytical approach to design, as well as a subordination of form to theme and the whole to its parts. The problem with delving into subjectivity during a time that has been characterised by a loss of idealism and innocence, however, as Umberto Eco and others have pointed out, is that it becomes necessary to temper emotion with some sign of recognition that this loss has taken place in order to be taken seriously, and that is where irony enters. Because of the realisation that society has devalued such a response, as well as the sensitivity and imagination that is necessary to make it, the mask of irony becomes a technique for making Romanticism acceptable, while also serving as a device with which to comment on a perceived shift in cultural values. This mask, which should not be confused with satire, nor be seen as the comic response to the tragic aspects of contemporary life simply allows its wearer to point out opposites. Rather than prompting ridicule, it encourages commentary, for while there may be an element of irony in satire there is little satire in irony. This Romantic tendency, which appears in many guises, is most obvious in the paradigms consistently cited by these architects in their work, particularly Neo-Classicist John Soane or Edwin Lutyens, who had such strong ties with the English Arts and Crafts Movement before the 1914-18 war, and fellow Philadelphian Frank Furness, who singlehandedly redefined the American response to Victorian Gothic, to name just a few.

If Romanticism is easily identified in these houses, their debt to the Renaissance is less readily traced, although equally present. Where the Arts and Crafts movement may have focused on an idyllic vision of the past, the Renaissance began with the resolve to recover a specific part of it, as well as with the intention of recapturing the humanistic ideals that were felt to be represented by that period of time.[1] The civic consciousness of 15th-century Florence can be identified directly with both the intellectual traditions of Athens and the institutional legacy of Rome, and when Raphael later painted *The School of Athens* as an allegory of that heritage, he conspicuously included the figure of Pythagorus in it, as a symbol of a continuing belief in a universal, numerical harmony.[2] With Andrea Palladio, who is another paradigm for these architects, the expression of that harmony also came to imply the use of symmetry. His *Quattro Libri dell'Architettura* of 1570 not only recast the Vitruvian standardisation of Classicism in the image of the proportional relationships that Palladio himself had established in his own measurements of ancient ruins, but also put forward a new system to replace it.[3]

The Mannerism that is frequently referred to by Venturi Scott Brown as an extension of this theme has perhaps been best described by Colin Rowe as 'an unavoidable state of mind'. He has gone on to say that, '16th-century Mannerism appears to consist in a deliberate inversion of the Classical High-Renaissance norm as established by Bramante, to include the very human desire to impair perfection when once it has been achieved, and to represent too a collapse of confidence in the theoretical programs of the earlier Renaissance. As a state of inhibition, it is essentially dependent on the awareness of a pre-existing order: as an attitude of dissent, it demands an orthodoxy within whose framework it might be heretical.'[4]

The struggle between what Rowe has identified as the Renaissance representation of public ideas, and the 'private literary flavour' of Romanticism, as well as the tendency to 'impair the perfection' of Modernist norms through the use of Mannerist strategies, is evident throughout all of the houses presented here, and may be seen in varying degrees in each of them.

They are declared from the start, perhaps beginning most clearly in the Vanna Venturi house, in the clash between the main entrance and the central hearth, which is deliberately placed in the path of entry to provide privacy for the interior. This conflict is further complicated by the insertion of a stair between the entry and the hearth, which is distorted by the demands of each. As in the Beach House that preceded it, this intentional dichotomy, once accepted, eventually seems to give the entire plan a focus. As Robert Venturi has described it: 'This house has a central core containing fireplace, chimney, and stair, as well as entrance. This is not a Classical configuration, because Classical plans usually contain space at the centre; but the core generates axial symmetry. The symmetry disintegrates however, at the edge, to accommodate particular requirements of the plan. We think setting up an order and then breaking it is in the Mannerist tradition of Classical architecture.'[5]

Such symmetrical considerations are also prevalent in the house in Greenwich Connecticut, of 1970, which, in spite of its apparent disregard for balance can be fit into a grid similar to that used by Palladio at the Villa Thiene at Cicogna, providing a tantalising hint that *The Mathematics of the Ideal Villa* might profitably be extended in this direction as well.[6] While its siting at the crest of a tree-rimmed greensward, as well as the unbuilt English manor house that was later proposed as an addition, would seem to argue for the predominance of a romantic aesthetic here, repetition of the 'broken order' seen in the Vanna Venturi house, as well as an inverted bow-fronted 'Palladian' facade tend to prevail.

A similar kind of duality is evident in the Trubek and Wislocki houses built in the same year on Nantucket. In this case, however, a local Wauwinet cottage type contends with the Classical influence, which is only subliminally present in the pedimented temple forms of both houses, as well as their inflected, conversational orientation towards the sea, which intentionally recalls the positions of Temples E and F at Selinunte. Rather than being organised along a longitudinal grid, each of these cottages relates to a cross axis, with the Trubek house stair breaking the symmetry more obviously than any such disruption in the plan of its diminutive partner.

A similar local prototype also governed in the planning of the house in Delaware, built in 1978, which is reminiscent of the barns that are common to the area. Like the house in Connecticut, it also commands a large, green, tree-lined site, and the bucolic, farm-like image that it conveys is further amplified with small details, such as a stylised garden trellis/pergola that acts as a gateway between the driveway and the woods beyond. Two overscaled lunettes, however, layered over the east and west elevations of the house, compete with this image, to superimpose a separate meaning of their own. While only the lunette on the western elevation uses an exaggerated, flat Doric colonnade for support, both arches are combined with a pedimented gable to evoke primal, basilican, forms that might seem totally extraneous to the rural idyll as first perceived.

While contradictory at first sight, the flattened Doric colonnade of this house, which initially looks like a caricature of the Order it mimics, actually answers to a nearby wood that comes close to the house at this point. In this way it is similar to the monumental order of the Temple of Poseidon at Paestum or the Heraion at Olympia, which both clearly show the evolution of Greek construction from timber to stone, and relate to their own natural surroundings. In a discussion of the relations between the column and the tree trunk, which was its original form, Demetri Porphyrios has used a comparison between David Humes' analysis of entasis in *A Treatise on Human Nature* with Le Corbusier's geometric view of the same relationship. As a conclusion to this Porphyrios has said: 'Both Hume and Le Corbusier speak of the way in which the column imitates the tree. Neither of the two speak of actually reproducing a tree. Hume discovers in nature's workings an anthropomorphic image. Le Corbusier, on the other hand, discovers in nature a geometricity which is made pertinent by his admiration for the precision and exactitude of the machine. The Classical imagination looks at the tree trunk and sees in it an image of stability which it commemorates in the form of the entasis of the column.'[7]

In the exaggeration of the entasis then, the essence of the natural beginning of the column is isolated here. Vincent Scully, who has so perceptively analysed the relationship between Greek architecture and landscape in *The Earth, the Temple and the Gods*, has recently identified this intention by saying: 'The columns are flat, breaking all the rules. They were round enough in the first sketches of the house, but Robert Venturi soon flattened them out, so taking up less space in the porch they define, but most of all, causing their sequence of planes to read as a thin screen and so as a continuation of the thinly sheathed walls that define the rest of the house. So the massive classical colonnade is turned into a vernacular shell, containing a box of space, but its units retain nonetheless the ghostly presences as the most archaic of all Doric columns, fantastic in entasis, wide and sharp in echinus. The flatter they are, the more they can be exaggerated in profile. The more startling they are as pure sign, no less than as wall.'[8]

In this sense, this arcade also recalls a particularly Albertian attitude towards the colonnade as ornament, rather than structure, as it was in antiquity. Whether it was determined to be this way through an intentional revision of Classical archetypes, as some would have it, or was the result of ease of access to late Hellenistic and Roman examples, the fact remains that Alberti did not view the column as an independent element, but as the loadbearing part of a solid wall, and the linear equivalent of a vertical line of force. The multivalency presented by this one part of the house in Delaware, where a single colonnade represents the exaggerated, vernacularised

shadow of nearby trees; an Albertian translation of an ornamental absence of wall; and the formal echo of the nostalgically rural typology embodied in the house itself; is indicative of the level of sophistication present in the exploration of these two themes.

As incongruous as the connection may seem; Venturi himself has stated that he sees his work as an extention of Modernism rather than the antithesis of it, and as such, his fascination with these themes places him within the tradition of German Romantic Classicism on the Miesian side of the movement, rather than in sympathy with the machine aesthetic of Le Corbusier.[9] In his sympathetic alignment with Schiller and Schinkel, rather than Chandigarh, Venturi extends the sympathetic humanistic strain of Modernism that is frequently forgotten today, and while Mies van der Rohe has now been faulted for his cold, anti-social minimalism in glass and steel, it should be remembered that the Carolingian Cathedral in his home town of Aachen remained a frequently quoted source in his early work, and he saw the New National Gallery in Berlin, which was one of his last buildings, as the contemporary parallel to the Neo-classicism of the Altes Museum.

Complexity and Confrontation

An unequivocal attitude towards the importance of the wall, as well as to the house as a shelter, rather than as a glazed pavilion exposed to the elements and public view, is especially evident in the early plans of the Wike and D'Agostino projects, as well as in the roof forms of Vanna Venturi, the Tucker house, and the ski lodge at Vail. This feeling for the protectiveness of the wall, in particular, has had a singular influence upon many architects today, who have generally tended to mistake introspection for living under siege and Mannerism for misanthropy.

An intriguing hint of such a reading, for example, comes from a joint statement by Thom Mayne and Michael Rotundi, who lead the Sci-Arc axis, appearing as the preface of a catalogue prepared for an exhibition of their work. In it, they say 'It is the *battle* or the *confrontation* which looms as one of the most fundamentally important points of departure from which we begin to understand how our projects develop. In much the same way that one can perceive life as a more or less constant confrontation with the complex and contradictory aspects of modern urban living, so can one perceive the evolution of a building. If the battles of life produce a richness of character, a depth of personality, and result in a final assessment of 'success' in life's experiences, then so do the confrontations dealt with in architecture produce a richness of building, a complexity of response, and an ultimately successful solution to the delimitations of site, client/programme and architecture.'[10] While such comments seem to stem from the 'tough times demand tough architecture' school of thought that is so fashionable today, their original source is obviously a bit more germane here, and if social antipathy may be seen to be one of the main reasons behind this current defensive design posture, such intentions are certainly not present in the Venturi Scott Brown houses. The consistent theme of conflict in these houses comes from the discrepancies that are frequently discovered between form and function in both plan and elevation, and are always consistent with the thesis of *Complexity and Contradiction*.

If these conflicts often seem disconcerting and possibly avoidable, they begin to take on a certain logic with familiarity; as is the case in the House in Tuckers Town, Bermuda, completed in 1975. The 'broken order' first mentioned by Venturi in reference to the Vanna Venturi house is repeated here, most noticeably in the shifted axis of the main entrance. In this case, the front door slides across the facade to accommodate the hierarchical claims of the library on one hand and the guest house on the other, which both share a vestibule with the main reception rooms in the centre. The angular contortions and intersections that result from this tripartite need also produce a house that is delightfully comfortable on its hillside overlooking the sea.

Two of the latest houses on Long Island (IV) and in Maine, are even more gracious, in the best Shingle Style tradition, both being reminiscent of the mansions designed by Peabody and Stearn, William H Dabney, Jr, or Mckim, Mead and White just before the turn of the century. Rather than being stiff formal exercises in this genre, which seems to have attracted the attention of several other architects recently, these houses evoke a genuine sense of nostalgia for an idyllic time in America's past, recalling straw hats and white linen, as well as long hot summer nights spent sipping lemonade on a verandah overlooking a vast expanse of green lawn. This is a dignified, rather than introspective or anti-social architecture which is particularly noteworthy in that it comes from the same office that first charted the course through the collapse of idealism for many in the past. While they have now taught generations of architects how to cope with this age of diminished expectations, Venturi Scott Brown have shown in these last houses that it is also possible, against all odds, to discover ideals once again, and the reasons for doing so defy the referential analysis that has typically been used to attempt to explain their intentions. The latest houses go far beyond the artificial creation of a heritage that has been so common in a comparatively young country that has always had such a craving for a history of its own. They mark a turning point at which America needs to be reminded that it is now in danger of losing the traditions that it has and they point towards the future by effectively reinterpreting the past.

Housing as Macrocosm

Because it is synergistic rather than additive in nature, multifamily housing is more than just a sum of its parts, presenting an infinitely greater problem to the designer than that of simply joining one dwelling unit to the next. Along with such difficulties, there is also the seemingly insuperable polemic of social responsibility surrounding housing, which, in spite of current protestations to the contrary, still manages to haunt some architects. For this reason, this book on 'housing' as well as 'houses' must contain what Denise Scott Brown calls 'paralipomena': concepts that have been excluded from architectural philosophies in the past.[11]

Those concepts begin to be evident with Guild House, which is as seminal to this segment of the firm's activity as the Vanna Venturi House is to their idea of the individual residence. While six storeys high, and designed to accommodate 91 apartments for elderly tenants, Guild House is compact and comprehensible, and is not an indulgence in the kind of monumental pyrotechnics that such a programme might have encouraged. And yet, in spite of severe budgetary restraints, there is a nobility about the building

that lifts it to a higher level. While fitting into its surroundings through the use of conventional materials, construction technology, and domestic symbols, Guild House manages to convey this higher level of intent through means that are far from accidental, and just as complex as those seen to be present in the houses just discussed. Although these means, such as the white line separating the bottom five floors from the penthouse, seem timid today, they were shocking when they first appeared, and have now been reproduced in magnified form, all over the world. Perhaps the most extensive, and effective description of Guild House has appeared in *Learning From Las Vegas* where it is compared with Paul Rudolph's Crawford Manor in order to elaborate on the theme of the duck and the decorated shed. As described in *Learning from Las Vegas*: the 'symbolism of the ordinary' includes 'the pretensions of the "giant order" on the front, the symmetrical, palazzolike composition with its three monumental storeys (as well as its six real storeys) topped by a piece of sculpture – or almost sculpture – [which] suggest something of the heroic and original. It is true that in this case the heroic and original facade is somewhat ironical, but it is this juxtaposition of contrasting symbols on one another – the appliqué of one order of symbols – that constitutes for us the decorated shed. This is what makes Guild House an architect's decorated shed – not architecture without architects.'[12]

Such intentions, as in all of the projects in this book, extend beyond mere appearances. They penetrate to the heart of a culture in which the unspoken ideal has always been the individual house rather than housing. In so doing, they establish a bridge between houses and housing by showing how significant elements in the morphology of one may be transferred to the other, how a generality of 'houseness' can be achieved by the individual house, and how each unit of housing can be designed as a home. The Learning from Levittown Studio notes included here take another sweep over the same plane, by reviewing architects' and merchant builders' housing, single houses and mass housing; from points of view both within and exterior to architecture. They suggest ways that architects can broaden their approach to housing yet remain architects and not become sociologists, or housers, or planners. In this sense, this study is a good primer on housing for architecture students, and should help them to incorporate difficult and problematic materials into their professional and artistic identities.

In trying to reweave architecture into the everyday environment and Modern architecture into the flow of history, Venturi and Scott Brown have also, in their houses and housing, hoped to break down the historical barriers that have separated the two typologies, and to show how a rapidly increasing social need may be addressed with dignity and invention.

Notes

1 For a counterpoint to this widely accepted view see John Onians, 'A Critique of Renaissance Historiography: Wittkower's Reconstruction of S Sebastiano in Mantua', *AA Files*, No 17, Spring 1989.
2 Rudolf Wittkower, *Architectural Principles in the Age of Humanism*, Academy Editions, London, 1988, p 119.
3 *Ibid*, Part II.
4 Colin Rowe, 'Mannerism in Modern Architecture', *The Mathematics of the Ideal Villa and Other Essays*; MIT, Cambridge, Mass, 1982, p 35.
5 Robert Venturi, 'Diversity, Relevance and Representation in Historicism, or *Plus ça change . . .* plus a Plea for Pattern all over Architecture with a Postscript on my Mother's House', the Gropius Lecture, Harvard University, 1982. Published in *A View from the Campidoglio*, Robert Venturi and Denise Scott Brown, Icon Editions, Harper and Row, New York, 1984, p 115.
6 Colin Rowe, *op cit*.
7 Demetri Porphyrios, *Classical Architecture*, Academy Editions, London, 1991.
8 Vincent Scully, 'Architecture: Venturi, Rauch and Scott Brown', *Architectural Digest*, March 1985, p 236.
9 Kenneth Frampton, *Modern Architecture: A Critical History*, Thames and Hudson, London, 1985, p 232.
10 Thom Mayne and Michael Rotundi, 'Architects' Statement: Morphosis', *A Decade of Architectural Confrontation*, exhibition catalogue of Residential Projects, 1978-88, Cheney Cowles Museum, Spokane, Washington, 1989.
11 Denise Scott Brown, 'Urban Concepts', *Architectural Design*, 1-2, 1990, p 6.
12 Robert Venturi, Denise Scott Brown and Steven Izenour, *Learning from Las Vegas*, MIT, Cambridge, Mass, revised edition, 1977, p 93.

I gratefully acknowledge the assistance of Denise Scott Brown in the preparation of this text.

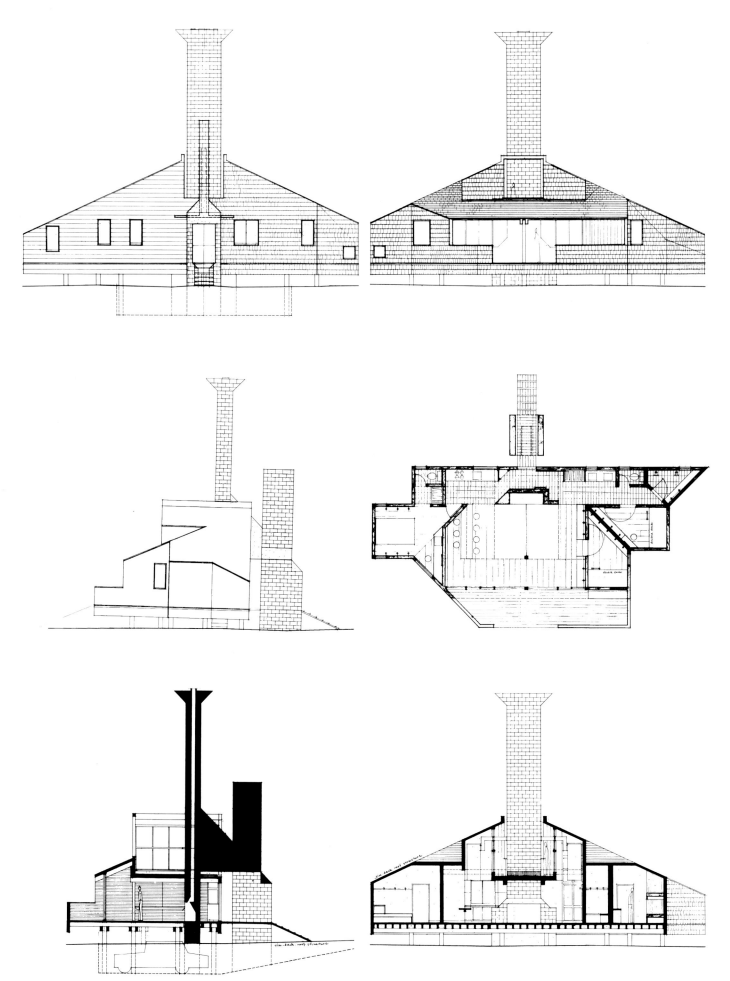

ABOVE: FRONT AND REAR ELEVATIONS; *MIDDLE*: SIDE ELEVATION AND GROUND-FLOOR PLAN; *BOTTOM*: CROSS AND LONG SECTIONS; *FACING PAGE*: MODEL

BEACH HOUSE, PROJECT, 1959
EAST COAST, UNITED STATES OF AMERICA

This weekend cottage, set among dunes on a beach, is to face the view of the ocean. It contains the simplest living accommodations, since the inhabitants are expected to spend most of the day on the beach. There is a small terrace on the ocean front and an open belvedere on the roof accessible by ladder and trap near the chimney.

The walls are balloon frame. The roof is wood-plank, toenailed so that the whole structure is a skin and a quasiframe at the same time. An exception occurs at the inverse clerestory and at the front opening, where the span is exceptionally long, and where there are some expedient frame members: one post and some beams. This exception at the centre makes the overall skin structure more apparent. (The floor is raised on wood piles and beams.)

Expressively, the house has only two elevations: the front, oriented towards the sea, and the back for entering. It has no sides, so to speak; and the front is different from the back to express its directional inflection towards the ocean view. The fireplace-chimney at the rear centre is a focus for the diagonal walls, which radiate, at first symmetrically, to form the inner spaces.

Because of these complex configurations in elevation and plan, the roof is hipped and gabled at the same time, and its original symmetrical form is distorted at the extremities of the building by varying interior demands, and by exterior requirements of orientation and view. At the pointed end, the exterior spatial-expressive demands of a house 'without sides', directed towards the view, dominate the secondary spatial needs of a shower inside.

The whole outside surface is natural cedar shingles. Barge boards at the juncture of the roof and wall are minimised to make roof and wall look more continuous. The overlapping scales of the walls end in a skirt over the piles. Windows and porch openings punch varying holes in the continuous skin. The interior surfaces, which you see beyond the windows and within the porch, are contrastingly painted board surfaces, like the inside lining of a cape. The soffits of the openings, where the skin is cut, are painted a contrasting colour. The shingles never touch the block chimney and its buttress, which divides near its base, and forms an open vestibule as well.

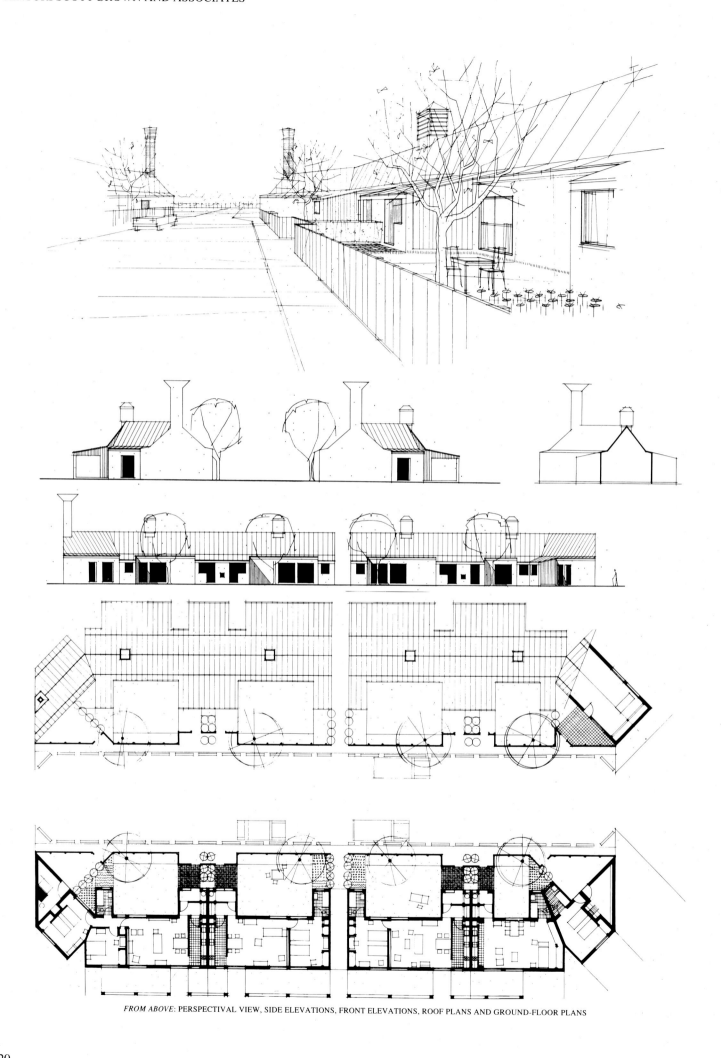

FROM ABOVE: PERSPECTIVAL VIEW, SIDE ELEVATIONS, FRONT ELEVATIONS, ROOF PLANS AND GROUND-FLOOR PLANS

FOULKEWAYS, GWYNEDD, PROJECT, 1959
GWYNEDD, PENNSYLVANIA

These are clustered attached houses for a retirement community. While the size of the individual units is small, there has been a great effort to keep the scale of the rooms large so as to accept people's furniture from previous homes. The gable and shed roofs preserve the image of a typical suburban home.

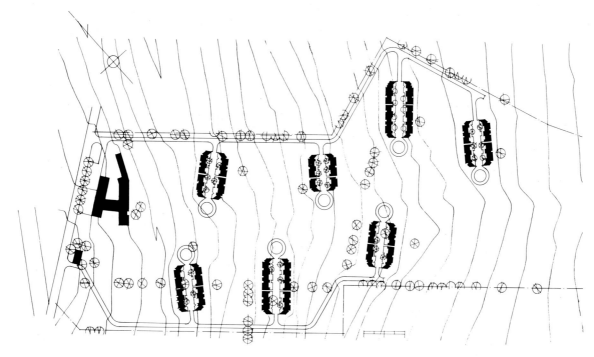

ABOVE: MODEL; *BELOW*: SITE PLAN

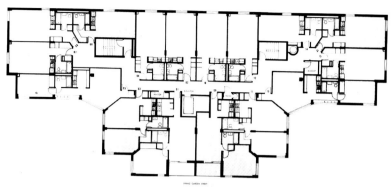

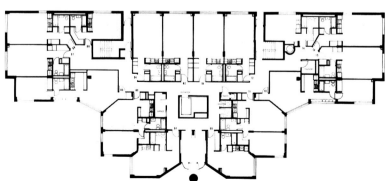

ABOVE: FIRST AND SECOND-FLOOR PLANS; *MIDDLE*: SIDE VIEW; *BELOW*: GROUND-FLOOR PLAN

GUILD HOUSE, 1961
PHILADELPHIA, PENNSYLVANIA

On a small urban site, this six-storey building houses 91 apartments of varying types for elderly tenants who desired to remain in their old neighbourhood.

Conventional architectural elements, particularly scale, were employed to accommodate budget constraints. The brick, an inexpensive red clay, matches an adjacent warehouse, but the brick nearest the sidewalk is of a different size from that used where the facade meets the street. The dark walls with double-hung windows recall traditional city rowhouses, but the effect of the window is uncommon due to their subtle proportion – unusually big. The scale of the windows also differs according to their distance from the street.

Interior spaces are complex to suit the varied programme of the apartment house. There is a maximum of interior volume and a minimum of corridor space.

The thin white line, suggesting the cornice level of a three-tiered building, looks timid now; it was horrifying then.

In *Learning from Las Vegas* this project is the protagonist of 'ugly and ordinary' in the debate with 'heroic and original' as represented by Crawford Manor, by the architect Paul Rudolf.

ABOVE: LIVING-ROOM; *BELOW*: MAIN FACADE

ABOVE: MAIN FACADE; *BELOW*: REAR VIEW

VANNA VENTURI HOUSE, 1961
CHESTNUT HILL, PENNSYLVANIA

This building is complex and simple, open and closed, big and little. Inside and out, it is a little house that uses big scale to counterbalance the complexity. Complexity in combination with small scale in small buildings creates a nervous 'busyness', whereas big scale in this small building achieves an appropriate architectural tension.

The inside spaces are complex both in shapes and interrelationships. The plan is symmetrical, but the symmetry is distorted at times to accommodate the particular needs of the spaces. For instance, two vertical elements – the fireplace-chimney and the staircase – compete, as it were, for central position. Consequently, on one side the fireplace distorts in shape and it and the chimney move over a little; on the other side the staircase constricts in width and changes its path because of the chimney.

In contrast, the outside form is simple and consistent, the front creates an almost symbolic image of a house. However, it also reflects the inside complexities through the varying locations and sizes and shapes of the windows, perforations in the outside walls, and the off-centre location of the chimney. The walls are layered to indicate enclosure yet punctured for openness. For instance at the main entrance, where the outside wall is superimposed upon the two other walls housing the stair, each juxtaposes openings of differing size and position, becoming layered space rather than interpenetrated space.

This house is a seminal work. In the years since its completion it has influenced other designs by the firm and the work of a number of other architects. It has been written about, studied and discussed extensively in print and in the classroom and is often visited by architectural students.

A Postscript on My Mother's House, by Robert Venturi, 1982

Although I am critical of much of the Classicism I see in Post-Modern architecture, and because I am frequently dismissed as a Pop architect, I would like to make it plain that I consider myself an architect who adheres to the Classical tradition of Western architecture. I claim that my approach and the substance of my work are Classical, and have been from the beginning of my career. My mother's house in Chestnut Hill Philadelphia, the second building of my design to be built, is an explicitly Classical building in the substance of its plan and form and in the ornament of its elevation. This was unusual in 1964, the year of its completion.

But the house, though Classical, is not pure. Within the Classical aesthetic it conforms to a Mannerist tradition which admits contradiction within the ideal order and thereby enhances the ideal quality of that order through contrast with it. To perceive the ideal you must acknowledge the real. Contradiction in Classical architecture, manifest in distortion and exception, occurs in the work of Palladio and many others who are my guides.

Some Classical and contradictory aspects of my mother's house are: the plan and the front and back elevations are symmetrical, about a central axis, but within the consistent perimeter of the plan, the extremities vary to accommodate exceptions in plan; and within the consistent profile of the elevations, the extremities vary to conform to exceptions within. The configuration of windows is asymmetrical, if balanced, for the same reason. The central core of the house is a solid, not the void typical of a Palladian plan. The solid core consists of a fireplace, chimney, and staircase, like that of a New England house of the 17th century. The central entrance reads on the front elevation as a void, rather big in scale like that of a porticoed Palladian villa, but it is contradicted by the blank, set-back wall of the solid core which is itself distorted in plan to accommodate circulation around it. Symmetry in plan is therefore modified at the extremities via exceptions, and nearer the centre via distortions.

The front and back elevation are Classically symmetrical with strong centralities. The front elevation is a Classical pediment. I derived this facade-as-pediment from the pavilion at the rear of Palladio's Villa Maser. A gable end as a front elevation was unusual in 1964. This gable is also a split pediment to reveal the central chimney block behind, to enhance the Mannnerist effect of spatial layering, and to make of the facade thereby a kind of disengaged sign. The facade as disengaged pediment or abstracted sign is also reinforced by the parapets of the front and back walls which make them seem independent of the roof and sides of the house. In the rear elevation the central element is the big arched window, less than a semicircle in shape. As in Neo-Classical facades, it promotes big scale and grand unity in a small pavilion.

Another unusual characteristic of this building for its time is its windows which look like windows. The sliding sash define holes in the wall in the traditional manner, rather than an absence of wall in the Modern manner. The horizontal cross muntin (a special element inserted within a standard Arcadia sash) depicts window through its association with traditional windows. This four-paned window with muntins – in manifestations large, small, sliding, awning, or double hung – is now a standard element of Post-Modern architecture.

Perhaps the most unusual feature of these elevations for 1964 was their applied decoration with its Classical character. There is a dado on the front and back elevations. It consists of a wood moulding placed a little high in terms of Classical precedent to enhance the scale of a small building. A shallow arch composed of the same moulding is applied above the entrance opening. The arch is juxtaposed on the concrete lintel that sits flush with the stucco wall. Arch and lintel together further enhance the scale of the already relatively big central opening. This use of ornamental redundancy and Classical association completes the Classical composition of the whole. The abstract linear quality of the Classical ornament applied to the smooth plaster walls, together with the disengagement of the walls at the parapets, makes the facades look almost like drawings and enhances their quality as representations of Classical architecture.

There are important elements of this design which are not Classical, for example the industrial sash and the strip window of the kitchen. But these act as counterpoint, they form part of the Classical-Mannerist element of contradiction within the whole and they establish this architecture as evolving Modern as well as reviving Classical. I did not explain this house as explicitly Classical in Complexity and Contradiction in Architecture *because in the 60s I was more interested in describing its Mannnerist than its Classical qualities. I did, however, make analogies with historical Classical architecture in my description of the building, and this has since become a Post-Modernist literary device.*

The Classicism that is essential to my mother's house is typical of most of the buildings I have designed. These buildings are more often Castle Howard-as-built, with the ultimate asymmetry of its north front, than Castle Howard-as-designed, with its unbroken symmetry; but they are Castle Howard nonetheless.

In the end I am speaking of a historicist symbolism that seeks the essence of a style – or a place, or a tradition. I hope that my mother's house achieves an essence of Classicism in its context; for achieving essence is our ultimate aim in using symbolism in architecture but that is the subject of another paper.

Some have said my Mother's house looks like a child's drawing of a house – representing the fundamental elements of shelter – gable roof, chimney, door, and windows. I like to think this is so, that it achieves another essence, that of the genre that is house and is elemental.'

'A Postscript on My Mother's House' is an extract from 'Diversity, Relevance and Representation in Historicism, or *Plus ça Change* . . . plus a Plea for Pattern all over Architecture with a Postscript on my Mother's House'. It was the 1982 Walter Gropius Lecture, delivered at the Graduate School of Design, Harvard University, by Robert Venturi and was first published in *Architectural Record*, June 1982, pp 114-115.

DINING-ROOM

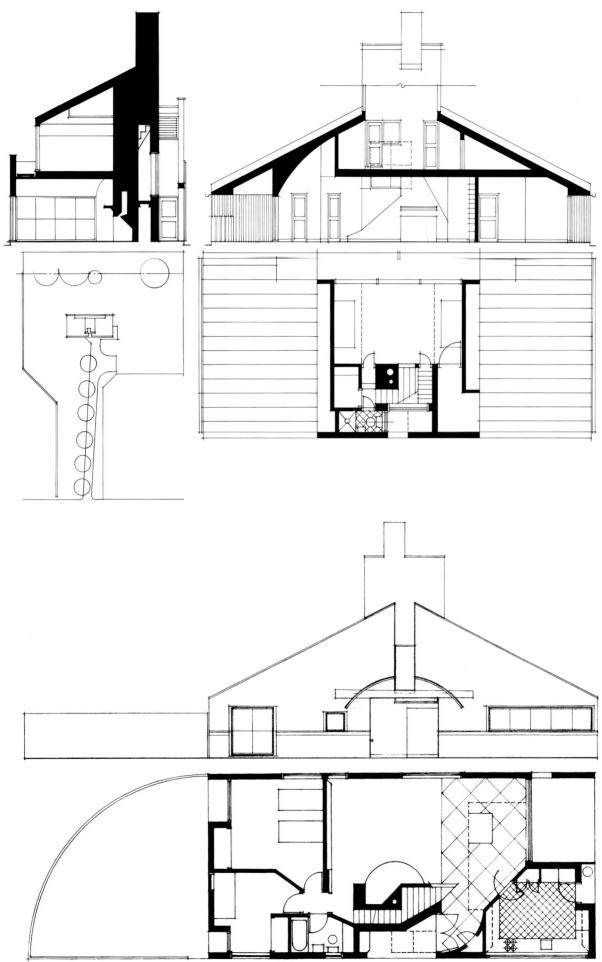

FROM ABOVE: CROSS AND LONG SECTIONS; SITE PLAN AND FIRST-FLOOR PLAN; MAIN ELEVATION; GROUND-FLOOR PLAN

ABOVE: 'NOWHERE STAIR' AND STAIR; *BELOW*: LIVING-ROOM

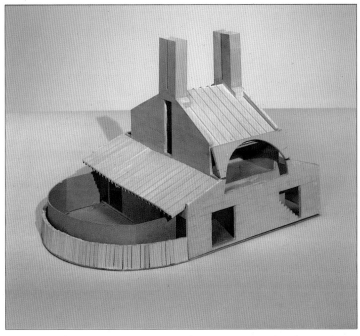
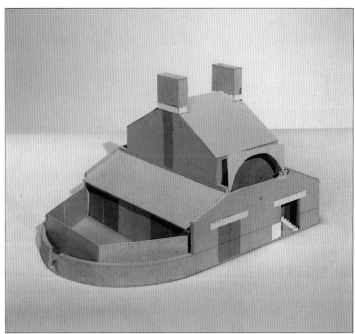
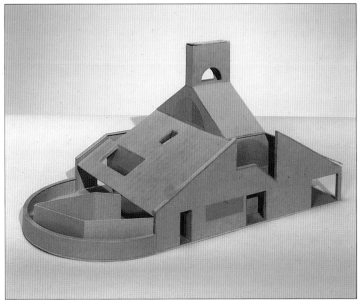

MODELS FOR PROPOSED SCHEMES

VANNA VENTURI HOUSE ADDITION, PROJECT, 1975

Conceptual sketches by Robert Venturi, considering the possibility of adding to his mother's house to accommodate a four-person family. The design approaches the generic problem of adding to a temple, and solves it by juxtaposing a second temple – a solution essayed earlier at Oberlin College and later at Bard College and, to some extent, Trafalgar Square.

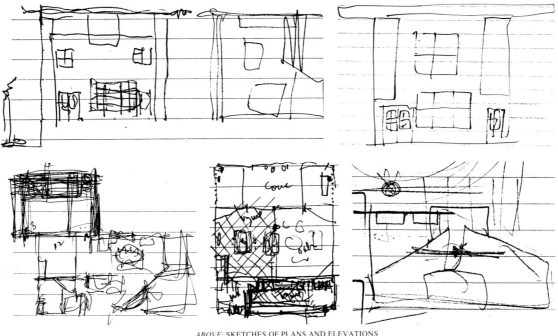

ABOVE: SKETCHES OF PLANS AND ELEVATIONS

MEISS HOUSE, PROJECT, 1962
PRINCETON, NEW JERSEY

The site for this house was a very large corner lot, flat and facing south towards the back with a view on to an old stable and a field of the Institute for Advanced Studies. It contained some patches of young trees and a row of old apple trees. The programme called for a large study for the professor, easily accessible from the front door and from his small bedroom; plenty of particularised storage space and an indoor swimming-pool, in addition to the usual rooms in a medium-sized house. The clients liked privacy and plenty of sun inside.

The composition is a duality. From the front it superimposes a long gable-roofed element on the back of a shed-roofed one. Essentially, the front zone contains entrances, circulation, storage, services, and a swimming-pool and it shields the back element, which contains the rooms for living. Upstairs in the front are two guest rooms, one of which the wife would also use as an office. The violent meeting of these independent roof forms seen from the front allows various clerestory windows for the shed-roofed back zone.

The duality is resolved by the perimeter, especially severe at the sides, which contains the two elements and contributes unity to the composition at this level. Also, in plan the back wall looking on to the long terrace is particularly complex in window indentations; which modify the sunlight or affect the interior space; in contrast with the severe front wall. The front wall's irregular window openings balance the otherwise over-symmetrical pediment facade. The wall in front, a third superimposed element, and the garage, slanted in plan to suggest an auto-court, imply enclosure.

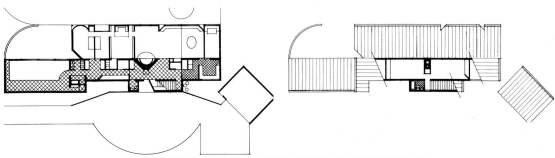

ABOVE: MODEL; *MIDDLE*: MODEL; *BELOW*: GROUND AND FIRST-FLOOR PLANS

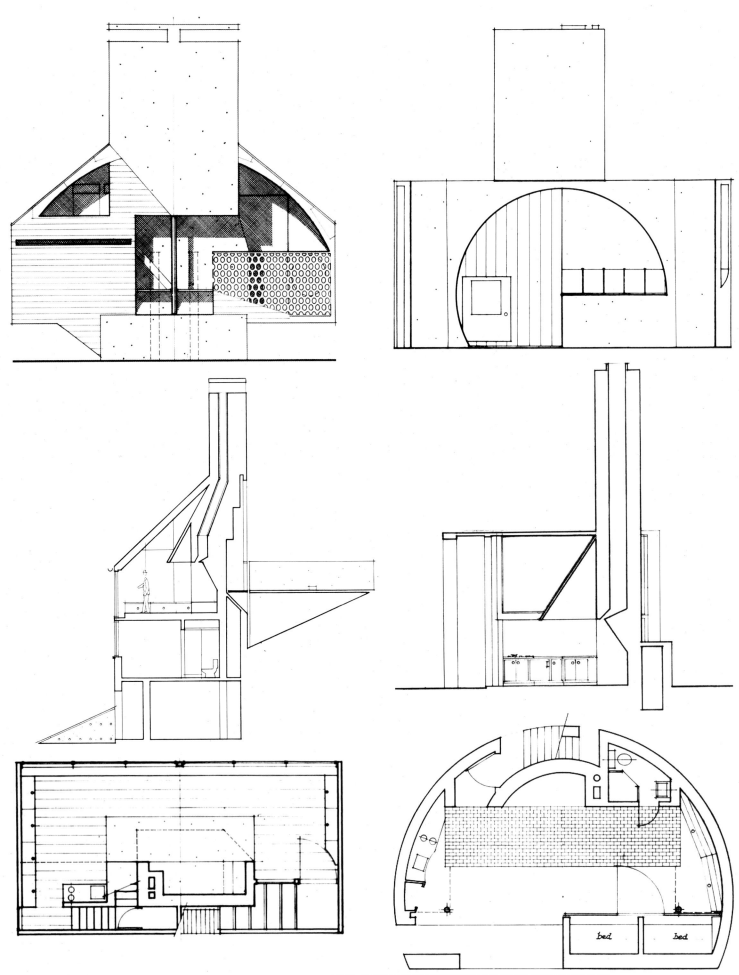

ABOVE: FRONT ELEVATIONS OF HOUSES I & II; *MIDDLE*: CROSS SECTIONS OF HOUSES I & II; *BELOW*: FIRST-FLOOR PLAN
OF HOUSE I & GROUND-FLOOR PLAN OF HOUSE II; *FACING PAGE*: MODELS OF HOUSES I & II

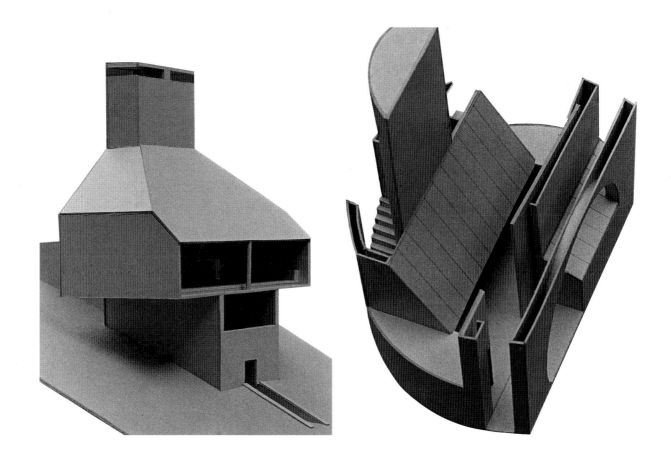

FRUG HOUSES I & II, PROJECTS, 1965
PRINCETON, NEW JERSEY

A project for a pavilion near a private swimming-pool to be used as a guest-house, dressing-rooms, and place for parties for the teen-age children of the family (thus the name – the frug being a youthful dance rage at the time). Our clients were friends with catholic tastes to whose exurban Cape Cod cottage we had added a colonial-style wing several years before, and for whom, previously, Frank Lloyd Wright had designed a Usonian manor on the same site.

Our first design was for the very steep and wooded site just below the swimming-pool. It was a shingled frame structure with a shed-hip roof ascending as a base for a big chimney. Inside, directed towards the chimney at the centre of the back wall, these roof pitches focused the space onto the fireplace, so that the little room, echoing in form the hood in plan and section, became almost secondary to its huge fireplace. But there is a counterfocus in this room opposite the fireplace and towards the outside: the exaggerated height of the hip is balanced by a very low eave in the front that forces the eye down to the beautiful stream below. Integral to the architecture inside is the built-in furniture of seats, counters and stairs that makes the little space less cluttered and breaks the symmetry of the whole. There is a bedroom and bath in the masonry base, and the approach is over a drawbridge. The

individual elements in this little house are big (the wide front door, for instance), and we have exaggerated the unity (almost every element inflects towards and is dependent on the fireplace and chimney) to give it the poignant monumentality of a little building with big scale.

Unfortunately this duckling was never built. The site proved too difficult and the design too elaborate. The second design located on the flat grade beside the pool is more like a shed. Its plan is a portion of a circle, it is a stuccoed block, one storey high (except for the dressing mezzanine), with a flat roof of wood planks. This building is also oriented beyond itself – in this case towards the pool. As in the first Frug House, the plan of the whole echoes the plan of the fireplace; the building is an extension of the fireplace. Its elements are big, and its furniture is built in, to decrease the formal clutter and increase the scale.

The eyes tend to complete the chopped-off circle of the plan suggesting a scale beyond the scale of the building. But the front elevation relieves the monumentality through the duality of the big sliding door. When the door is open in the summer for a barbecue, the sleeping bunks are covered and accessible through a door in the door. The door in a door is the entrance in the winter.

VIEW OF HOUSE AND BEACH

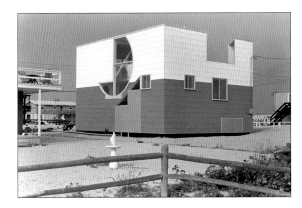 

LIEB HOUSE, 1967
LOVELADIES, LONG BEACH ISLAND, NEW JERSEY

The Lieb House is an ordinary shed with conventional elements: it uses asbestos shingles with imitation wood-grain relief, which was once the indigenous building material on Long Beach Island. And it uses big elements, such as the staircase, which starts out as wide as the width of the house and gradually decreases to three feet on the first floor. However, its unconventional elements, when they do occur, are explicitly extraordinary, as in the big round window like a 1930s radio loud-speaker. It is a little house with big scale, different from the houses around it but also like them. It stands up to, rather than ignores, the environment of utility poles.

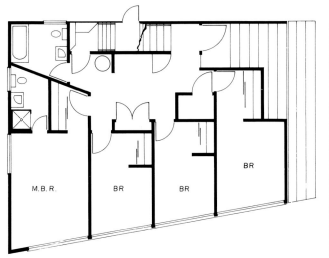 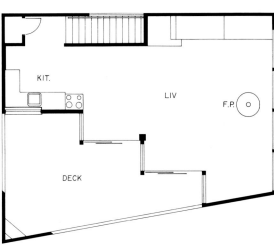

ABOVE: REAR AND SIDE VIEWS; *MIDDLE*: LIVING-ROOM AND CLOSE-UP OF ENTRANCE; *BELOW*: GROUND AND FIRST-FLOOR PLANS

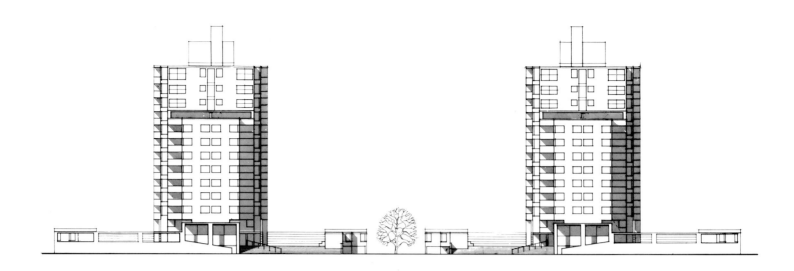

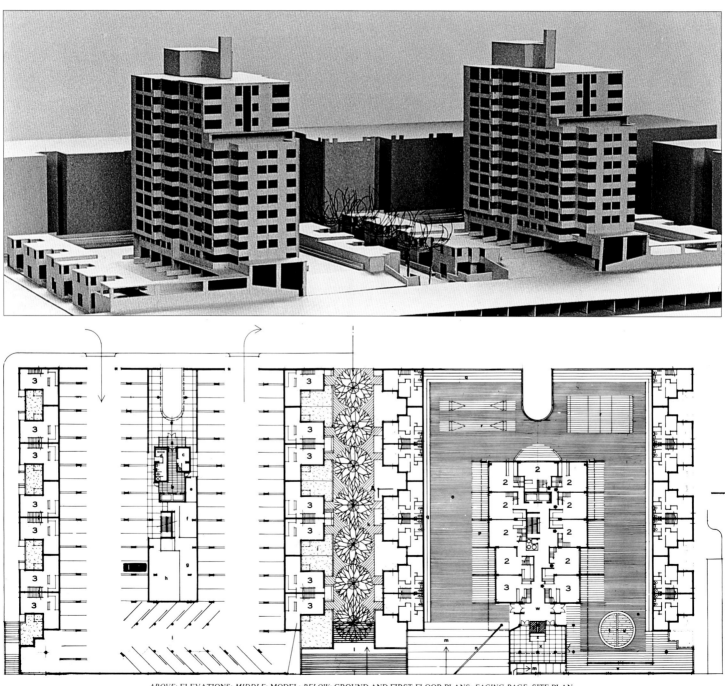

ABOVE: ELEVATIONS; *MIDDLE*: MODEL; *BELOW*: GROUND AND FIRST-FLOOR PLANS; *FACING PAGE*: SITE PLAN

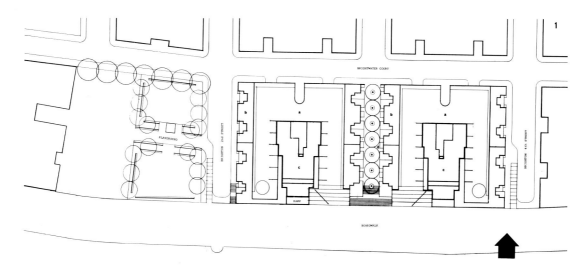

BRIGHTON BEACH HOUSING COMPETITION, 1967
BRIGHTON BEACH, BROOKLYN, NEW YORK

The programme for a two-acre site on the boardwalk in Brighton Beach, Brooklyn, specified a certain ratio of apartment units within 2,800,000 cubic feet with covered parking in accordance with local zoning specifications. The design for this site was to be a prototype.

We designed two modified slabs perpendicular to the shore to allow a view of the sea and to cut off the view as little as possible from housing blocks behind. The project included houses with gardens, a common recreation area and parking. The slabs were stepped, in plan and elevation, to inflect them towards the view. The configurations of the common spaces were to encourage communication among the tenants.

This design is not based on a 'megastructure', 'Habitat' or other system that depends for its implementation upon a technological revolution in the building industry or a change in the living patterns within the society. We have tried, using today's construction systems and financing methods, to show how a pleasant living environment can be integrated into an existing neighbourhood, augmenting the quality it already has.

Although it has two towers, this is not two projects, since the duality of the two blocks is resolved at ground level. The street connecting the two halves is a positive element: an interior beach road for the sea-going public, a civic space as well as a private one. The ramps and sun decks facing the boardwalk are also public, intended to act as a meeting and greeting place between building and boardwalk, and as a visual amenity for residents and boardwalkers.

The terrace space on the boardwalk is designed primarily for the old and the very young. All access is ramped; the handrail across the main ramp leads the user up a gentle diagonal. The pathway from the common room to the boardwalk sitting areas contains no steps. Sitting areas, both indoors and out, face onto

the boardwalk, yet receive shelter from the sun.

Philip Johnson commented on the project in Learning from Las Vegas *(first edition, 1972) by stating:*

This jury is indicative of many problems in today's architecture and deserves full discussion and publicity. To the majority, of which I was one, [the Venturi and Rauch-Kawasaki submission] seemed a pair of very ugly buildings. We felt (the majority consisted besides myself of Messrs Abrams, Sert and Ratensky) that the buildings looked like the most ordinary apartment construction built all over Queens and Brooklyn since the Depression, that the placing of the blocks was ordinary and dull. The forms that the buildings took were, in our eyes, deliberately ugly. There were some obvious merits: the town houses set around the cul-de-sac of the street, and the extension of the boardwalk surrounding the base building. But these minor virtues seemed to us overwhelmed by the all-pervading ugliness .[. . .]

The first prize winner strikes me as a rich and satisfactory solution.[. . .] The general conception . . . pleased us all. First, a tower (which may have to be lowered) on the west, facing the existing park. Second, a six-storey surrounding group that semi-encloses a multilevel court. [. . .]There are hardly any innovative features in this design. It could have been designed at any time in the past 15 years, but its excellence in the handling of the grammar of our time is praiseworthy.

Philip Johnson called our entry ugly and ordinary. At the same time Gordon Bunshaft call our Transportation Square project ugly and ordinary. This made us understand some essence of our own work, which we termed ugly and ordinary and analysed as such in Learning from Las Vegas.

HOUSES OF ILL-REPUTE
ROBERT VENTURI AND DENISE SCOTT BROWN

Housing is good, but houses are bad. This has been a maxim of Modern architecture. While it is true that concentrating on individual houses is socially irresponsible and technologically irrelevant in the context of the continuing housing crisis of our time, within the circumstances of architectural practice as it is for the individual architect, the little house should not be scorned. It is still the first job for most architects, for obvious economic and social reasons: architecture is an expensive medium, therefore conservative clients award big commissions to old architects or big firms. (Ironically, big responsibilities often go to young planners and to young architects in big firms.) The little house for a close friend or relative is usually therefore a first opportunity for the young architect to test theories and expand them. If times are slack, this at least allows the beginning architect to put heart and soul and a full work week, into developing this one small idea, which is always a deepening experience. And if the client is poor, the years spent refining the plans while waiting for financing can be in the nature of a personal odyssey for the architect. Of our earlier houses, our beach, mother's and frug houses were, to some extent, odysseys. The Lieb house was an early attempt to use a home builder's vernacular in a not-altogether vernacular way.

Norma Evenson has described how in the 20s the young Le Corbusier theorised about La Ville Radieuse while doing little houses which he considered the formal prototypes for later urban-scale work of social and technological significance. However, although Le Corbusier saw his individual villas as prototypes for industrial housing, his models and those of Modern architecture in general have only slightly influenced mass housing – at least developers' housing in America – and American architects are still uninvolved in housing. This we believe is due to the unreal outlook Le Corbusier and his followers brought to the problems of housing; but it does not preclude the possibility that the individual architect, working sympathetically with merchant builders' real needs and constraints, their real

media and symbols, cannot fulfil today (or at least share with others) the paradigmatic role that the architect has perhaps arrogantly claimed for himself.

Designing a house may also be the only opportunity for architects to work with real user-clients as opposed to a corporate committee or public agency, and therefore to deal with the irrationalities of emotional needs and values. The richness of this experience is what they must later depend on (although in the context of different value systems) to eke out statistical data when working on housing – at least for most projects and before 'community architecture' brought representatives of user groups into architectural decision making. However, situations are rare where more-than-lip-service is paid to community participation, or paid at a level that gives architects real information on users. So depending on individual rich clients' emotions to tell you something about collective poor clients' emotions, although imperfect, is often better than nothing.

In the career of an architect, a project for a house can serve as a punctuation and a point of departure – an opportunity to seclude oneself and focus one's thinking; to be able to control the whole in a way that distils and clarifies, and informs the bigger work at hand. The houses illustrated here were such exercises.

Our descriptions of them rely a good deal on historical analogy, because the use of historical models was important in their development and is therefore helpful in describing them (but not because we think it is necessarily the right method for all architects or for seeing all issues and solving all problems). We unashamedly lift our analogues from their historical context – picking out for study perhaps only one aspect of their make-up – to create new comparisons, aid analysis and goad invention. This traditional methodological device seems to bother some architects but few historians.

The original version of this article was published in *Learning from Las Vegas* (first edition, 1972)

SIDE VIEW OF MODEL

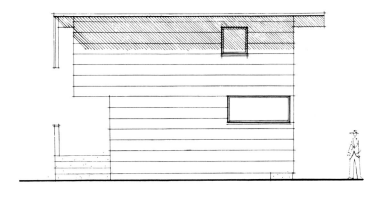

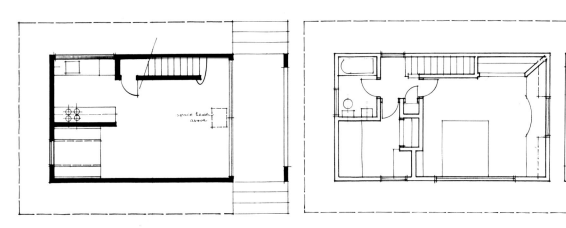

HERSEY HOUSE, PROJECT, 1968
HYANNIS PORT, MASSACHUSETTS

This is literally what we have designated elsewhere as a 'decorated shed' and as an appropriate stance for most architectural problems today. To explain: a 'decorated shed' city hall would be a conventional loft building, designed for the flexible interior uses of present-day bureaucracies, with rhetorical meaning applied on its outer surfaces in the form of a big sign blinking, 'This is a Monument'; this stands in contradiction to what we have called a 'duck' – that is, a nominally undecorated building, itself distorted into a vast decoration through the contortion of structure and function, to serve an unadmitted decorative aim.

Our house is a beach cabin for a small family on

Cape Cod. It is a simple box of asbestos shingles with a flat roof and the proverbial Mary Anne behind. We applied ornament to the front porch to increase the scale of the facade: the circular opening suggested by the curve of the lattice above and the rail below extends beyond the sides of the facade and includes both storeys – like the giant order on a Classical portico. We hoped to achieve thereby a poignant shed, both little and big, dumb and sophisticated – after all, it was a cabin for a Yale professor. It is hard for an architect to design a dumb building but we think we succeeded. Unfortunately it was not dumb enough (or we were not clever enough) to meet the budget, and it didn't get built.

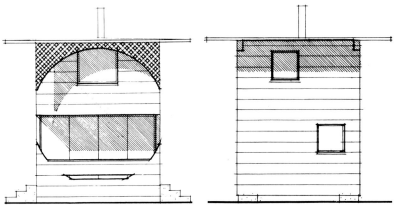

ABOVE: SIDE ELEVATION; *MIDDLE*: GROUND AND FIRST-FLOOR PLANS; *BELOW*: FRONT AND REAR ELEVATIONS

39

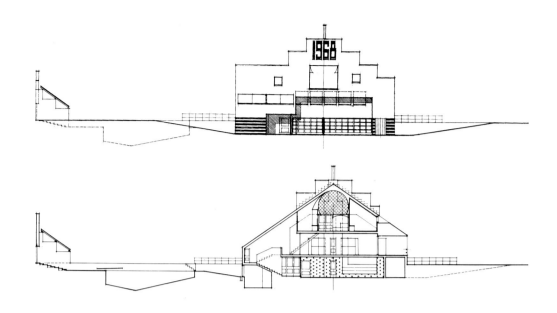

D'AGOSTINO HOUSE, PROJECT, 1968
CLINTON, NEW YORK

This is an admitted 'duck' for a unique programme, a rural site and a generous budget. It was for a couple who wanted to enjoy the varied views surrounding a beautiful plateau in northern New York State. The main floor is therefore raised half a level above grade with opportunities to see out all around. The house is made of grey glazed brick to match the colour of the weathered planks of a barn nearby. The facade towards the long approach forms a bold silhouette with a stepped parapet reminiscent of Dutch architecture. The bold scale must accommodate the automobile as well, since the garage is the usual entrance in this snowy climate. You enter therefore into a 'beautiful' garage (white glazed brick with black headers) onto a 'grand' stairway and up to the piano nobile, *as if from the carriageway of an 18th-century Neapolitan villa rather than via a mean garage into a back door in the kitchen. The sunken auto court has sloped sides to facilitate snow ploughing and the swimming-pool, sunken too, to protect bathers from prevailing winds, is on a side axis, recalling the sunken gardens of a George Howe Norman house. The pavilion at the end of the pool is a little parody of the big house. The bedroom on the top floor is vaulted in wood – Polish synagogues of the 18th century.*

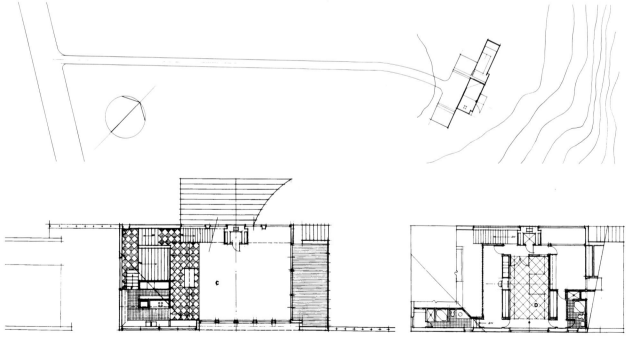

FROM ABOVE: MAIN ELEVATION; LONG SECTION; SITE PLAN; GROUND AND FIRST-FLOOR PLANS

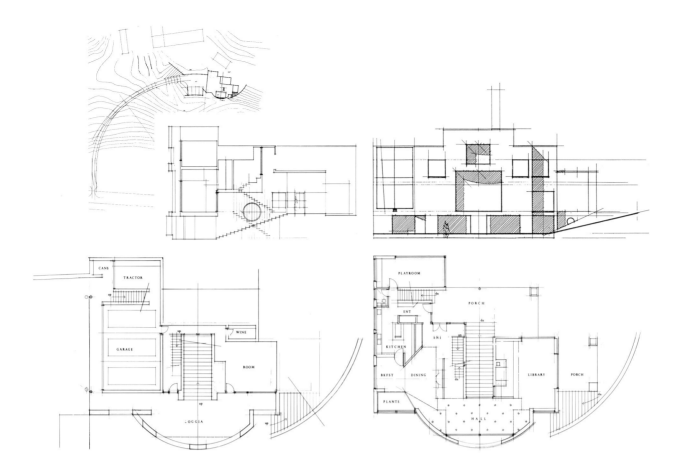

WIKE HOUSE, PROJECT, 1969
DEVON, PENNSYLVANIA

Another 'duck' that significantly won't get built because the housing market in suburban Philadelphia abounds in good, old, big houses. Our clients found a beautiful Queen Anne manor, circa 1931, on 12 acres, about the time we firmed up the estimate of our schematic design, and they naturally bought the manor because it was twice the size of our design and one-third the price. The programme for this family with three small children and a live-in children's nurse was Lutyens-like in scope: a central hall for entertaining, only a little narrower than the gallery at Syon (but considerably shorter), one-and-one-half storeys high, shallowly vaulted and spanning the long way, and with a window facing the central exterior stair well. There is a library remote from the children, a breakfast room with a south-east exposure for plants, and a kitchen which, despite the Edwardian complexity of the plan, was to control the entrances and dominate the main

floor almost in the manner of a Usonian 'work space'. The clients wanted a 'formal' setting for their 18th-century antiques and therefore the plan starts out symmetrically. Note particularly the venturi effect of the exterior stair, which splits the house from the lower loggia in the front to the upper entrance in the rear (you have to fight your way into this house). We made the front of the house like a bold Vanbrugh manor with deep shadows to be read from the road down the hill. The auto-entrance facade, with its rectangular geometry of big, frequent windows, is like an Elizabethan manor house, but without the symmetry, and the back, with its functional accommodations to inside needs and the swimming-pool play area outside, is pre-TAC Gropius. Facades were to be yellow brick like Holkham Hall. The porch side and the back were to be frame construction clad with flush boards painted the same colour as the brick.

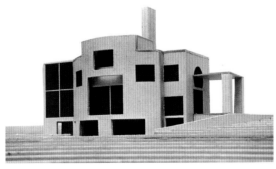

ABOVE: SITE PLAN, CROSS SECTION AND FRONT ELEVATION; *MIDDLE*: GROUND AND FIRST-FLOOR PLANS; *BELOW*: MODEL

FROM ABOVE: WEST AND EAST ELEVATIONS OF THE WISLOCKI HOUSE; GROUND-FLOOR PLAN, NORTH ELEVATION, FIRST-FLOOR PLAN, SOUTH ELEVATION AND CROSS SECTION OF THE WISLOCKI HOUSE; NORTH, EAST, SOUTH AND WEST ELEVATIONS OF THE TRUBEK HOUSE; PLANS AND LONG SECTION OF THE TRUBEK HOUSE

THE TRUBEK AND WISLOCKI HOUSES, 1970
NANTUCKET ISLAND, MASSACHUSETTS

Houses for another Yale professor and family, and a related family; the larger is complex and contradictory, the smaller is ugly and ordinary. The position of the small house blocks the sight of the neighbour's house to the west. The side elevations of the large house have windows like other windows in the house but much bigger: their sills are 4'3" high to enhance and obscure the scale. These are 19th-century Wauwinet fisherman's cottages with Shingle Style and Art Nouveau complexities inside. They are also two little temples on the plain, by the sea at Selinunte, with three bigger-than-usual porch steps in front to sit on.

ABOVE: VIEW OF WISLOCKI AND TRUBEK HOUSES; *BELOW*: LIVING-ROOM OF TRUBEK HOUSE

HOUSE IN CONNECTICUT, 1970
GREENWICH, CONNECTICUT

This house was for a very young couple who were New York cosmopolites, close friends of Andy Warhol, and inspired collectors of Pop Art and French Deco furniture of the 20s and 30s. The house was to contain these works of art, and some fine examples of American antique furniture, in an easy way that did not emphasise their display. The site consisted of 30 acres of rolling green landscape and included an existing stable.

The clients called for relatively few but generous spaces – no separate dining-room, no entrance hall, and the garage is near the entrance, reflecting an informal way of life dependent on a minimum of domestic help. The style of the house is Modern in that it has a flat roof, strip windows, aluminium sash, cantilever construction, and no overt historical symbolism. On the other hand, the flat roof is reminiscent of that of a Georgian country house, as is the near symmetry of the facade, whose central focus is reinforced by ascending roof heights, a hierarchical window composition, and a flat curve in plan. The stark setting on a manicured lawn resembles that of a Classical manor in the 18th century, yet the quasi-Classical main facade refers to the anti-International Style Moderne style of the Art Deco furniture within. On the exterior, green glazed-brick walls with a dash-striped pattern make this the first building in the so-called Post-Modern period with an all over, polychromatic, decorative pattern. This element has been disregarded by critics because Modernists find ornament distasteful and Post-Modernists find this ornament anti-Classical. The use of green makes the house striking symbolically – green is an unusual colour for masonry architecture – but recessive formally, in the verdant context of the Connecticut landscape.

The interior, too, contains decorative elements that symbolise Art Deco styling – black and white marble stair risers, a checkerboard floor pattern in the entry, and pendant cove lighting and indirect natural lighting in the dining niche.

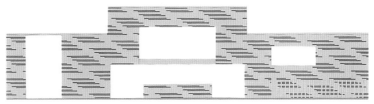

OPPOSITE: DINING AREA; *ABOVE*: SIDE VIEW; *BELOW*: ELEVATION SHOWING BRICK WORK

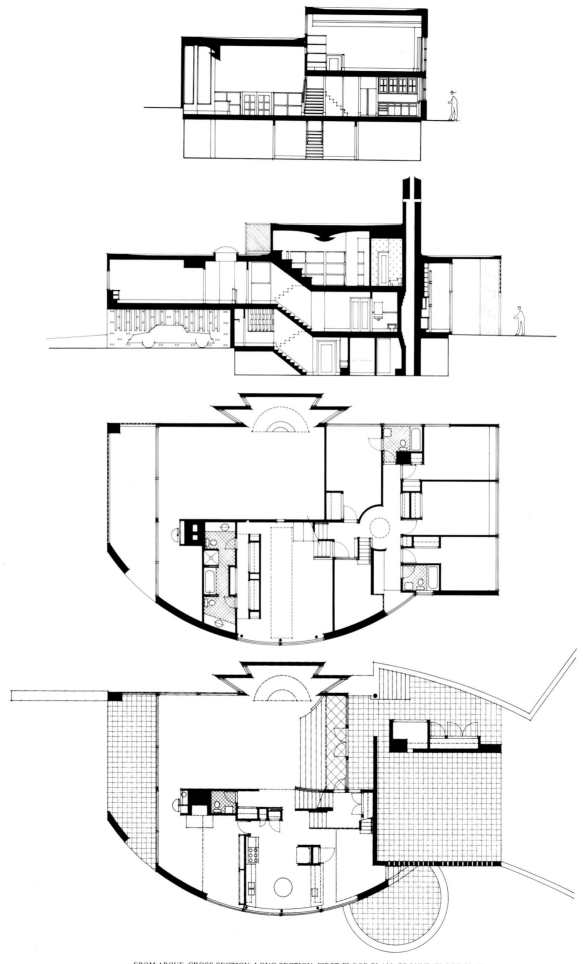

FROM ABOVE: CROSS SECTION; LONG SECTION; FIRST-FLOOR PLAN; GROUND-FLOOR PLAN

ABOVE: REAR VIEW; *BELOW*: LIVING AREA

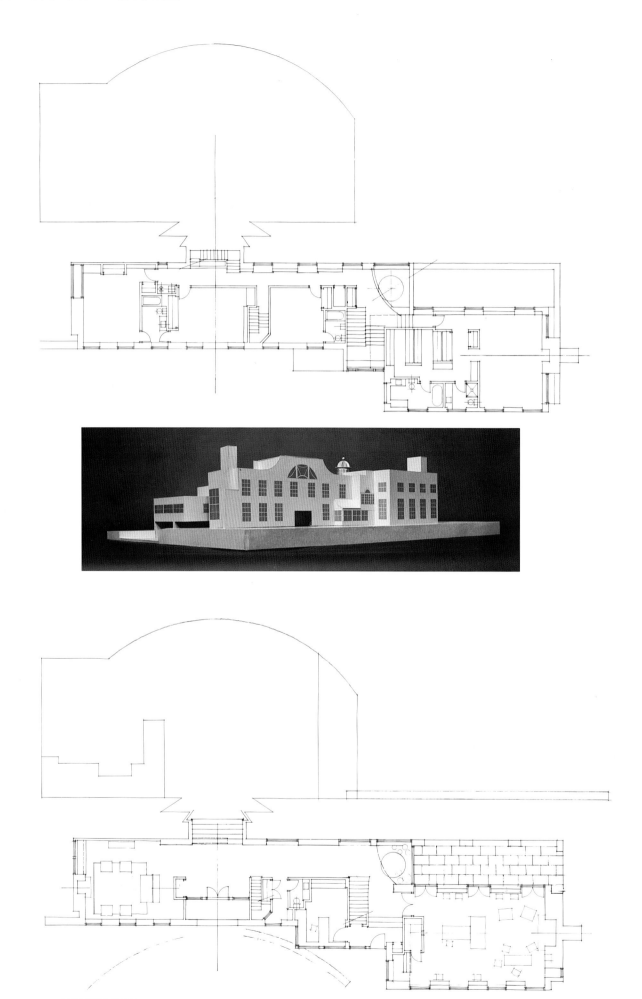

ABOVE: FIRST-FLOOR PLAN; *MIDDLE*: MODEL; *BELOW*: GROUND-FLOOR PLAN; *FACING PAGE*: FRONT AND REAR ELEVATIONS

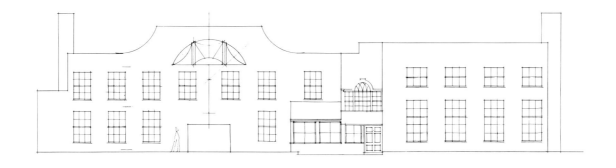

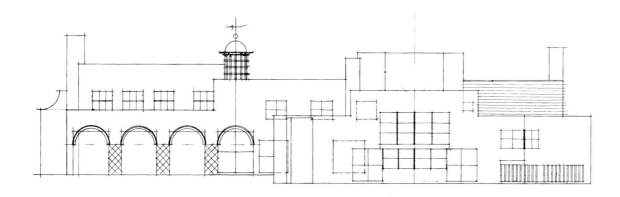

ADDITION TO THE HOUSE IN CONNECTICUT, PROJECT, 1976

This project was commissioned because the family had grown in size with the arrival of triplets. The parents had diverted their collecting to American antique furniture and American primitive painting. They had intensified their interest in horses to include breeding, polo, and racing, and now had large new stables under construction. They had also changed in more subtle ways, towards a lifestyle of greater formality.

Specific requirements for the expanded houses were extra bedrooms for family and guests, more service space, a proper dining-room, a formal entrance hall with reception room, and a garage remote from the house. A big library was to be added for an extensive collection of books on horse breeding and equestrian sports, and for informal entertaining.

We saw this addition as a challenging opportunity to create a building complex in the easy way the English modified and added to their country houses, over generations, in different architectural styles, and particularly like those houses with Georgian fronts and Elizabethan behinds. Because the original house was frontal in layout, it was easy to place a red brick Georgian facade behind it. From the original front you would then see a Mannerist juxtaposition of a green

brick form against a plane of even, red brick bays. This permitted an interior of some formality, but it created as well a degree of idiosyncrasy in plan which was in the vein of another English great-house tradition.

We located the new entrance in the addition so the new wing would dominate as you entered. To promote architectural formality, we created an exterior forecourt at the entrance and on the central axis of the old house. A cross-axis penetrating the entrance hall formed a long gallery connecting the reception room at one end with the library at the other. The living-room in the existing house became the new dining-room, at a slightly lower level, on axis with the new front door. Kitchen and service in the existing house remained where they were. New bedrooms were on the first and partial second floors of the new wing.

The new wing of red brick was rather literally in the style of a late 18th-century manor, its chaste but grand form contrasting with that of the existing house. As a long and narrow element blocking the old house from the entrance court, the new wing was mainly one facade, a two-dimensional sign – in the end, an expansive gesture.

ABOVE AND BELOW: LEVITTOWN FACADE AND INTERIOR

REMEDIAL HOUSING FOR ARCHITECTS STUDIO
DENISE SCOTT BROWN

Following the **Learning from Las Vegas Studio**, *another, called* **Remedial Housing for Architects** *or* **Learning from Levittown** *was given at Yale in 1970. It became the basis for an exhibition called* **Signs of Life: Symbols in the American City** *held in the Renwick Gallery of the Smithsonian Institution in Washington, DC in 1976. The programme for the Studio and the 'Home' section of that exhibition are reproduced here.*

The housing problem is beyond the nostrums of architects. From the mid-50s to the mid-60s the US averaged about 20,000 units of public housing a year. Since then, with social upheavals, this figure has increased to 50-60,000 units. Britain last year built over 120,000 units. The US builds fewer houses *per capita* than most large Western nations, including Russia. Meanwhile there are 135,000 families on the waiting list for public housing in New York City alone. This studio will be an attempt to relate ourselves as architects more realistically to this problem than we have done in the past.

Social concern was an important part of the early Modern Movement in architecture and mass 'social' housing one of its dearest topics. Nowhere have the architect's claims and interest been greater yet nowhere has his impact been less. Fifty years after the first calls to reconsider the social tasks of architecture, 'social' housing as dreamed of in the manifestos is non-existent in America, and housing for the poor, much more narrowly defined as public housing and the various aid programmes, is provided, as we have seen, in ludicrously small quantities. To most architects 'residential work' means the design of houses and apartments for the rich. On the other hand, the mass home building which does exist in America and reaches a broad range of the population above the poverty level, happens without benefit or apparent need of the architect and is, indeed, scorned by him, as 'grey areas' and 'urban sprawl'.

Architects do, however, figure prominently in urban renewal programmes. These are ironic simulations of CIAM social housing – ironic because they look somewhat like the projects discussed by idealistic hotheads in Athens or Otterloo but house instead not merely the rich, but the comparatively very rich. Urban renewal has played a now well-known part in achieving the opposite of the earlier architects' aims, dislodging and dispossessing the poor in the name of urban progress; but sophisticates know better than to blame the architect; the fault lies more broadly than that, and the agonising now going on in the profession together with a great flailing out in new directions is testimony to an architectural will to improve. However, if the new will is to succeed it must channel itself in more useful directions than those given it by the early Moderns, and the architect's level of awareness about certain ignored but relevant aspects of American housing must be increased. We architects have had a set of not too useful attitudes in housing with regard to: industrialisation; economic possibilities; political possibilities; people's values and attitudes; people's life-styles; the value of architecture to society; 'total design'.

The first on this list is still, even in these days of advocacy planning, the first panacea considered by architects (and not only the mega-structure boys). We guess that it is probably the last problem not the first that should be considered, and follows easily upon the solving of some others. The last on the list has been found to be no panacea except, ironically, in Caesar's Palace, Las Vegas and maybe Trafalgar West, Houston, where 'total design' melds with 'styling', and what is being 'totally designed' is not a mega-structure of 'anonymous', industrialised units, but an image and a way of life – and horrifying to architects. In between in our list are areas of great ignorance for architects and some where they and they only can make important contributions.

This is therefore to be a remedial studio (for us and our parents). Its view is not comprehensive but biased; biased in the opposite direction from where we came, in order to reassert a balance. We shall be more interested in what people make of their housing than in what the architects intended them to make of it. We shall be more interested in the iconography of 'Mon (split-level, Cape Cod, Rancher) Repos' than in the iconography (*or* structure) of the Dymaxion house or Falling Water. We shall be more interested in the marketing of industrialised house components than in their design. This is not a course in Housing, but an examination of the field from an action-oriented and architectural point of view, designed to make a subsequent, deeper study of housing more meaningful. We shall not be involved in civic or community action to do with housing in this studio, but in learning what is needed to make our professional contribution to this action more relevant.

The work of the Studio will fall into three phases. At the end of each there will be a class presentation and discussion:

Phase I UNDERSTANDING (4 weeks) Housing economics and politics, programmes and policies, attitudes and life-styles – the construction industry, case studies and comparative studies: a great deal of reading, some lectures and a series of group reports describing these phenomena and their local manifestations in New Haven.

Phase II ADDING (6 weeks) Broadened by our immersion in the library we can now add to the knowledge of housing some inputs which social scientists find difficult to deliver and which architects have not until now found relevant: knowledge on attitudes of people to the physical qualities of housing – its appearance and symbolism, its functional arrangements and its location. A critique of architects' attitudes to housing and its design. Architectural analyses of the 'sprawl' environment from a non-judgemental point of view.

Phase III CREATING (3 weeks) The main emphasis in this studio is on knowledge and understanding, adding to ours and the field's. But it is an action-oriented knowledge, suited to professionals who are hoping to make their actions useful. In the last few weeks we shall begin to think about the use of this knowledge, synthetically and creatively: in the design of a suburban area which includes low-income residents; in a regional strategy for low-income housing in New Haven; in the design of new roles for architects to fit new ideals and a new situation, and in an artistic reinterpretation of suburban residential artefacts – doing for houses what Oldenburg did for hamburgers.

Studio Organisation
Our Studio is in 165 York and our lecture room is in the basement of 165 York. There are, in addition to the critics, two teaching assistants, Peter Schmitt and Bruce Heitler. A series of visitors will meet and talk with us as work proceeds. Students entering this studio are required to give all their semester credits, bar one course's worth, to the Studio. We shall all meet together for all lectures and presentations, and shall meet in small groups to discuss work in progress. Meeting times

each week will not be regular but will be scheduled and posted in advance. The assistants will be in New Haven all week, the critics an average of two days a week.

Two members of the class will be co-opted each week to serve as class organisers, for whatever needs to be done.

Members of New Haven city agencies have expressed a willingness to help us in studio. However, in the interests of maintaining this spirit of co-operation all semester, we have promised we would not inundate them with calls for help. Requests to city agencies must therefore be made through the teaching assistants, not directly.

Reading and Library
A bibliography has been prepared for this studio. In addition three books are considered texts and can be bought at the Co-op:
1 Douglas, Paul H (Chairman), *Building the American City,* National Commission on Urban Problems, Washington 1968 (paperback).
2 Kaiser, Edgar F (Chairman), *A Decent Home* The Report of the President's Committee on Urban Housing, Washington 1969 (paperback).
3 Bellush, Jewel and Murray Hausknecht (eds), *Urban Renewal: People, Politics and Planning*; Anchor Books, Garden City, NY, 1967.

STUDIO RHA: Phase I: Understanding
This is an intensive reading and research phase. During the next month you should read 10 to 20 books and articles carefully and become well acquainted with the contents of perhaps 50 more (see bibliography). The research topics divide our subject into portions manageable by one to three people; the presentations, which will be written, oral and graphic, are a means of sharing the information. For each topic you will be asked to relate what you have learned to:
1 The New Haven SMSA (using city data and metropolitan data).
2 Low income housing.
3 The architect's product and his role in housing.
We hope to use the New Haven data during Phase III.

RESEARCH TOPICS
1 Housing Economy (10-13 people)
An economy is a social arrangement whereby resources, goods and services are produced, allocated and distributed and levels of well-being, positive and negative, are achieved. A market can be thought of as an arena in which, or a mechanism through which, demand and supply, asked price and bid prices are mediated. Today, in the market for new housing, Adam Smith's 'hidden hand' is given a big assist by government, through its various programmes from mortgage insurance to urban renewal, and, to a lesser extent, by large scale developers; but the poor and to some extent the architects, are still able to compete in only very limited sectors of the housing market. The housing economy is complex and varied; more so than either the urban designers or the mathematical model builders understand. It provides something acceptable for most, though not all, people. But the market for habitats, unipods, and even high art architects' houses is quite small at the moment and, barring an about face on the part of the culture, is likely to remain so.
a) Housing Market (2 people)
In any city there are not one but several housing markets. If I am an engineer with three kids, employed in suburban New Jersey, I am not (bar some hanky panky) in the market for an apartment in downtown Camden. If I am a retired school teacher who until now has lived with a niece in West Philadelphia I will not turn up next in a mansion in Ardmore. If I am a black mother of six on the waiting list for public housing my opportunities are limited to the dilapidated houses of the inner-city.

What are the factors which put people into different housing markets? How are housing supply and housing demand described and measured? How do large scale developers test and in other ways determine their market? And planners? What are the main housing markets in New Haven today? Describe briefly the characteristics and size of each, and try to account for its existence in the New Haven SMSA. What markets are missing or unimportant in New Haven and why? What minimum yearly income does a New Haven resident require to enter the new housing market at its lowest level? Who lives in old houses and who in new? How does a stock of old houses affect the market for new?

Are there trends which may alter the present market patterns in New Haven?

To what extent are architects involved with each of the markets you have described?
b) Housing Capital Costs (1 or 2 people)
If I want to build a new, single family detached dwelling with a yard, I can't locate it on Rittenhouse Square, unless I am a multi-millionaire, and crazy. So the housing market influences location as well as type of house. The two dimensional pattern of activities on the land which results from a family's or firm's need for accessibility mediated by their ability to pay for it, is called the space economy by regional scientists and urban land economists. Describe some of the early theories of the space economy which seem pertinent to the location of housing.

Describe recent computer models which simulate a housing market and which can eventually be mapped on the land. What variables do they include? Which do they ignore? How do they deal with intangibles such as amenity, which seems important in people's choice of housing?

Describe and graphically depict the spatial distribution of the housing market in New Haven. Where do the poor live and why? In what areas are architects' housing to be found? Where do architects live themselves? Analyse the location decision behind Charles Moore's choice of a house on Elm street.
c) Housing Capital Costs (1 or 2 people)
Land, site-works, professional services, construction, construction mortgage, closing costs, transfer costs – what are all the costs faced by the developer and buyer of a new house, apartment, mobile home and so on? What are all the costs faced by the buyer of an old one? Give these costs for different housing types in different locations in New Haven. Make a large chart of the information showing it in a comparative way by unit, type, location, etc. Include public housing and other forms of subsidised housing. How are capital costs affected by different forms of house finance? How do construction costs figure as a percentage of total costs for different housing types? Where in the total cost picture are the best possibilities for cost savings? How do costs relate to scale of development? How do architect designed projects compare in cost with those of merchant builders? How do merchant builders, private rehab builders and public housing costs compare and why?
d) House Operating Costs (1 or 2 people)
Rates and taxes, plumbers and electricians costs, the lawn mower, etc: at what point do all these become so onerous that I decide to move into an apartment at $350 a month including operating costs? Probably the decision between home ownership and renting is never made on the basis of operating costs alone. But at what price level and for what types of housing would a home-ownership policy for public housing save the authority enough in rent collection and maintenance expenses and worries to make it worth considering? At what point does a landlord abandon rather than maintain (or under-maintain) a slum house? What are the main operating costs for a home-owner, mobile home owner, apartment building owner, housing authority, for old and new housing? What are these costs for different segments of the housing stock in New Haven? What is the calculus upon which a private landlord bases his rents? How does this differ for a non-profit housing group? For a public housing authority? Compare the rents paid by members of the Housing Economy team. What factors account for the differences?
e) House Financing (1 or 2 people)
My apartment in an IM Pei tower rents at $230 a month. In the Oskar Stonorov public housing towers visible from my window the rents are between $27 and $65 a month. These projects have roughly similar building costs and very different financing arrangements though both have government subsidies. The monthly payments on my suburban home will vary considerably depending on whether it is conventionally or FHA financed.

List the ways in which new housing is financed privately, publicly and through a mixture of private and government sources. Give examples of each in New Haven. Show how rates and terms of mortgages affect prices and carrying charges for a new house and a small project.

What are the private and governmental financing arrangements available for the buying and rehabilitating of old houses? Why is it easier to buy a new house than to buy and fix up an old one? Explain the rehab versus rebuild argument. How do tax laws affect the relative advantages of home ownership and renting? In what sectors of the market is financing unavailable or exorbitantly high? What determines the supply of funds available for mortgage loans? Why are mortgage interest rates so high at present?

f) Non-market Aspects of the Housing Economy (2 people)

It is sometimes said that the government should be the houser of last resort, the provider of free, decent, safe and sanitary housing for those who cannot afford to pay. The US has a worse record on this score then any other Western, industrialised nation, and, ironically, may assist and directly subsidise the rich and middle income groups, through various policies from tax rebate and urban renewal to the low-middle income programmes, more than it does the poor.

List all the ways from tax policy to public housing that the government assists and subsidises housing, and list these by level of government. Try to get some idea of the magnitude of this subsidy by type in New Haven. How many dwelling units are there in New Haven? How many have received each sort of subsidy? How many housing starts were there last year in New Haven? How many received each sort of subsidy?

g) The Housing Stock (1 person)

This means the total of all dwellings in an area. List the ways in which the US Census describes the characteristics of the supply. List other ways of describing the stock.

Make a detailed tabular description of the housing stock in the New Haven SMSA by different characteristics. Show how it has grown and changed over time. What characteristics are most useful to planners, urban designers and architects, as a means of describing the stock?

Who owns, controls and manages various sectors of the stock, particularly the inner city rented stock?

2 Housing Politics (2 or 3 people)

By politics we mean as much the politicking, pressuring and lobbying that takes place at a national, state and local level as the voting which happens later in the legislative chamber. When the head of the National Association of Real Estate Boards testifies in Congress against public housing; when the mayor goes to Washington and Roy Wilkins goes on television; when a local group of outraged citizens flings verbal brickbats at a Redevelopment Authority or threatens to boycott local department stores if a freeway plan is adopted – these are political actions which may or may not have the desired effect on policy.

From your readings on power structure, political decision making and social process and protest, name the main protagonists, individual and group, public and private, in policy decisions on housing in New Haven (not forgetting John Q Public, who votes with his dollars and his feet). Illustrate their interaction by documenting the decision-making process and the decisions made over several questions of housing policy in New Haven. (Grigsby says this is impossible; do the best you can.)

Where do architects and planners come into the process? Comment on the role of the architect as 'professional', 'expert', 'value-free technician', 'gatekeeper of information', 'message bearer between protagonists', 'social leader and innovator', 'leader of the team', 'guru', 'artist', 'prophet', 'advocate planner', 'member of the chamber of commerce', 'member of a government agency', 'student', 'servant of the establishment', 'upper class gentleman', 'middle class intellectual', 'most eligible bachelor in the women's magazines'. Comment on possible roles for architects and students in the housing issues you discuss.

3 Programmes and Policies (2 or 3 people)

The advocate architect who delves into lists of available housing programmes, breaking his head against the unrememberable numbers, 235, 236h, 221d3, by which the habituated describe them, comes eventually upon the scandal that they mask: that there is tragically little to spend to house the poor, since most 'programmes' have been approved but not funded, or some which were relatively successful have later been dropped in favour of 'better' ones promised for an unspecified future time. Meanwhile the stormy situation induced by the shortage continues. We are told, however, that more can be done with programmes and policies as they are, by imaginative people, which is an adequate reason for getting to know them; in any case knowing them is a prerequisite for changing them.

The Philadelphia Housing Authority made a citizens' guide to housing programmes in Philadelphia which ranged from federal housing aids to local building, zoning and planning codes and to the help available from various private and public institutions in the city. Can you find or make your own, necessarily briefer, but annotated list for New Haven? How have these programmes influenced residential building in New Haven? From your readings discuss the importance of the major programmes, ie, those most useful in getting or most harmful in hindering low-income housing.

Make suggestions for changes in and additions to both private and public programmes. Can you think of others, ommited by the PHA which are important to housing, such as taxation, research and development?

Implicit in many governmental codes and programmes are attitudes to the house and the residential environment. Zoning comes immediately to mind as a means of maintaining the property owner's image of self *in situ*, but there is also the relation between FHA regulations and the look of Levittown. Expand this speculation in a general way in preparation for more specific consideration in Phase II.

4 Attitudes, Life-styles, Social Conditions (5-7 people)

We are trying to get at qualities of people, singly and in groups, that influence housing and decide its nature: quality of life, way of life; cultures and subcultures; high, middle and low culture; ethnic, socio-economic and age groups; readership groups; recreation patterns; consumption patterns; social preferences; social roles; life-styles; slum and suburban ways of life (merely lower class, working class and middle class?); male and female differences; urbanism-familism differences; local-cosmopolitan differences; regional differences. Here we are asking for a broad view which will give us a framework for our attitude studies in Phase II.

a) Taxonomy (2 people)

We have started a disordered classification system for this topic above. Can you, from your reading, expand it and order it into some form of matrix suitable for relating to housing?

b) Illustrated Descriptions (1 or 2 people)

Produce a set of illustrated descriptions of several different American life-styles, some from New Haven and surroundings, others from elsewhere, based on your reading. Couch your descriptions mainly in terms of life in the neighbourhood and home. Don't choose only exotic ones. Illustrate your own as a pilot project. Next, define yourself as the total of your roles (student, taxpayer, husband, social being, consumer) and describe your home as a stage set for role playing.

c) Emerging Life-styles (1 person)

Hippie communes, students' shared households, teenagers moving out on their own, Leisure Worlds, Swinger Versailles – which are fads and which may be important for the future? Describe and illustrate some emerging American life-styles, as in b) above; add prognostications on how they might develop in the future. Don't choose only exotic examples; nevertheless, pay special attention to adolescents as indices for the near future (as in Duhl in *Planning for Diversity and Choice*, Anderson ed)

d) Attitude Research (1 or 2 people)

This is a preparation for our own research work in Phase II. How do you discover people's attitudes? The two main ways are by asking them and by observing them. Both are subject to error. Asking, because, among other things, it presumes a relationship between what people say they will do and what they actually do; observing, because it presumes that observed behaviour in environment X can serve as an index for future behaviour in that environment. The devising and conducting of surveys which avoid these errors demands more skill and more time than we have available. Therefore we shall depend to a large extent on the surveys of others for the 'asking' aspect of the work; and in the 'observing' aspect, concentrate mainly on people's actions on and depictions of the built environment; what housing choices they make, what they do to their house or what parts of it are reproduced in the press or on TV for what reasons.

Expand our classification system of ways in which attitudes are determined and comment on those which will be most useful to us in the Studio. Make a bibliography of sources of information on attitudes towards housing and get as many of your sources into the Art and Architecture library as possible. To do this range widely from Madison Avenue to the School of Business to the Survey Research Center (University of Illinois) to local builders and their trade journals, to *Life*, *Time* and the *New Yorker*, to TV, to Oldenburg and Keinholz.

Make a preliminary reconnaissance in the New Haven SMSA to determine which residential areas would be suitable for our own field studies. Bring back photographs.

5 The Construction Industry (2 people)

Make an extended list of the members of the construction industry. Make this broadly defined, to include all those who come into the picture from the time the client announces 'I want to build,' until the time he walks in the front door. Mark what constitutes the construction industry as it is customarily defined. List the various types of contractor who form the home building industry, by housing type (single family dwelling, apartment, mobile, systems, etc) and size (in units produced per year). How does each type structure the elements of the narrowly defined construction industry and relate to those in the broader definition? How do his size and organisation relate to what he builds?

Describe the organisation and operation of several home builders in New Haven. Where are possibilities for cost reduction in the home building industry? How did Levitt effect savings? What kinds of economies of scale can be achieved through mass production in the house building industry? How much is 'mass?' Architects habitually define the construction industry as highly inefficient and 'medieval.' Some economists (including Charles Abrams) suggest that it is not. What, from your reading and studies of this topic, do you feel? What are the prospects for the adoption of the mass produced, avant-garde building technologies dreamed of by Archigram or Safdie? Or by Ehrenkrantz? Or GE?

What will be the effect of the entry into the city-building field of the large oil and appliance companies – Sun Oil, Gulf, GE?

Why does no one build new housing cheap enough to suit the pockets of half the nation?

6 Case Studies and Comparative Studies (2 people)

US: Columbia, Reston, Levittown, Trafalgar West. Other countries: housing in developing areas (especially John Turner's for Peru) new towns and housing projects in Europe. History: Georgian London, US Stick and Shingle styles, and 'streetcar suburbs.' Here our interest is not in a spatial analysis of the housing (though we'd like to know what it looks like) but in how it got built, that is, how everything we've studied in topies 1-5 conspired to bring it about. Set up a framework for describing your examples which will make comparisons possible.

Format

You should be prepared to give a 15 minute talk on your chosen topic illustrated by slides, maps, schedules, tables, diagrams and sketches. You should prepare a condensed version of your report (typewritten, same format as ours; 50 copies) which contains the information, verbal and graphic, that the rest of the class needs for the following phases and to take away with them. Since ability to address a multiple client, a citizens' group, a mayor's committee takes on a growing importance in community architecture, where 'advocate' often means 'spokesman,' we shall lay stress here in making this presentation – spoken, written and visual – a professional job.

Approach

If you were asked to find out all about dental science in an afternoon, you would hardly start out with the dental students. We suggest you approach your topic with the gaiety of despair. There is much more here than you can do in a month. In a fragmented and fast moving civilisation one learns how to use partial knowledge. You should understand the scope of your topic and some of its specifics in depth. Should you become a 'houser' you will need to know more; from Phase I you should learn at least this, and where to go for help.

STUDIO RHA: Phase II: Adding

The last few weeks have been an intensive search for sophistication in housing along paths not commonly frequented by architects. The next phase, the longest, is based on the premise that there is a professional contribution to be made to housing in an area – the physical qualities of the residential environment – where social scientists flounder and where architects, because of aesthetic and authoritarian hang-ups, have scorned to tread or trodden only very narrowly, chasing their own shadows. Liberated from these hindrances, perhaps we can do pioneer work, not on some architectural utopian frontier, but here in the existing urb (and sub-) among existing values and life-styles.

We shall be documenting attitudes, architects' included, and analysing the urb, particularly residential 'sprawl' of different eras and areas. To do so we shall range from real people and real sites, to the mass media and Madison Avenue, to 'straight' literature in the library and to 'literatures' which have housing content.

RESEARCH TOPICS
I Attitudes (8 people)

We are concerned now not with general attitudes but specifically with attitudes to the physical qualities of housing and its environment. We have described these as: attitudes to appearance, symbolism, amenity and the expression of social meanings through architecture; attitudes to functional uses and functional arrangements of elements of the house and housing environments; attitudes to housing location.

Here are some questions which a documenting of attitudes could be expected to illumine:

How high a value would different people (by age, income, life-style, etc) in different housing (by type, price, location, etc) give qualities and attributes such as ample space, privacy, aesthetics and styling, individuality, newness, security, nearness to work, sense of community, neighbourliness, community facilities, class identity and the expression of status?

What would a low income population require of suburban housing? What problems will suburbanites' attitudes cause if low-income housing is built near them and are there possibilities of reducing these problems somewhat through 'styling' to suit both groups? What would suburbanites require of low-income housing near them?

What is a 'home?' How does the image of home vary by subculture, housing type, image source? What is the image of public housing?

What are the elements of various house interiors and house environments? How does the use of these elements reflect life-styles and values? What do different people in different houses want to use a house for? What improvements might they suggest for different house and environment types, both in functional arrangements and to suit their life-styles? Can you detect changes in how people use houses? Are there new recreational needs in and around housing? Are status definition requirements changing? Comment from your findings, Beyer's *Housing & Society* and the house plans that go with them. How do your findings agree with those of Handlin? ('The System of the Home', *Connection*, Spring 1969.)

How do our sources cover low-income and slum housing, if at all? And architect housing?

These are just a few of the questions which can be asked. They suggest that each survey must cover the three attitudes not merely in general but by life-style, housing type and perhaps other variables. The Phase I Life-style 'Taxonomy' will help to give an order to this enquiry. Meanwhile the simplest way of breaking down our task is by research material source and by two-man research teams.

a) Surveys (2 people)

This involves asking people (questionnaires) watching them (user behaviour studies) talking with builders and salesmen and studying other people's surveys and polls such as those of academics, the census, market analysts, developers, architects, Madison Avenue, Gallup, consumer researchers.

Since survey taking is a skilled and lengthy task, we should stress the analysis of existing surveys over making our own. Our bibliography lists as many surveys as we could find. Phase I Topic 4d 'Attitudes Research' will list others. For the rest you are on your own and should consult with the expert surveyors and pollsters mentioned above. Use photographs, movies and words to produce comparative information from all your sources which illumines the attitudes listed above and the questions asked about them.

Comparing your behaviour analyses with your questionnaires, can you find differences between what people *say* they want in housing and what they appear to want from their actions? From your experience comment on 'gripe and fantasy needs' and on 'value trade-offs'. Are there differences between what the architect intended and how the users see and use his project? Try to make your data from various survey sources comparable, then comment on the different findings based on different survey goals. How do these 'biased' assessments of need compare with architects' biases and with your own empirical findings? By April 2 you should know and have classified your 'secondary' survey sources and should be planning your small 'primary' researches, their venue, nature and limits.

b) Sites (2 people)
Housing and residential areas (by type, location, age, etc) 'Model Homes', interior decorator stores and displays, furniture store windows, other store windows, thrift shops and flea markets.

A photographic and movie survey, perhaps a photo-essay, with some rigorous way of arranging material comparatively (à la *Learning from Las Vegas* building type schedules?) and with conclusions drawn in words, would be helpful. Structure your programme to throw light on the three types of attitudes and on the questions asked in the introduction to this topic, above.

Is there a universal house type in New Haven (like the Philadelphia rowhouse) which, over time, has been used by different groups in different ways? Document the elements of house facades in New Haven neighbourhoods, by class. We recommend Route 130 north and south from Camden for lurid 'swingles', also Fairless Hills, PA (near Bristol) also Levittown, PA for people's alteration of housing over the years, to suit themselves – is there a correlation of alteration type by house price? How do the functional uses and arrangements and image of a house vary from Hamden to the Hill to 'Swingers-on-Sea' to New Canaan, Conn, to Levittown, PA? Are there changes in the intensity of imagery by house type, era and area? If so, why? Use book sources (*Hollywood Style* by Knight & Elisofon) to cover sites you cannot visit. What sites suggest what the housing preferences of the poor might be if they were less restrained economi-

cally?
c) Blurbs, Ads and Journals (2 people)
Content analysis of developers' blurbs, billboards, mass transit ads, newspaper real estate sections and ads, mass magazine ads, women's magazines contents and ads, Sears Roebuck catalogues, *House & Home*, *American Builder*, *Mobile Homes*, *House & Garden Building Guid*e (see bibliography for further listings of trade journals; don't miss 'how to sell it' articles in builders' magazines) interiors mags, architecture mags and charities mailings. A photo-essay, using rigorous methods of analysis, description and comparison to answer the kinds of questions about attitudes asked above.

How does the image of a house vary from *Time* to the *New Yorker* to *Scientific American* to *Mechanics Illustrated* to *Rolling Stone* to *Daily News* to *McCalls* to *P/A*? How do promoters describe content – a 'Betsy Ross bay window' etc – verbally and in images? Find out from developers and vendors of house plans which models sell best, where and to whom. Which product ads use a home setting to sell their products? How do these homes differ by product and by magazine? Use your best sociological insights to speculate à la Handlin on the elements of the ad and why they were put there. Do admen have estimates of the effectiveness of their backgrounds for their purposes? Have some products' ads shifted away from the home? If so, why? How do NAACP, SCLC, blurbs show homes of the poor? In content analysis a set of categories is chosen which fits the various sources and the material is broken down by these categories for comparability. Can you devise a set of categories for our sources?
d) Electronics and Celluloid (2 people)
This involves analysing TV ads, soap operas (*Peyton Place*, *The Forsyte Saga*) documentary and other shows which have residential scenes; movies by type, and the preparation of a photo and movie essay using rigorous methods of analysis, description and comparison to describe the three attitude areas and to answer some of our questions about attitudes.

What TV ads use house backgrounds? How do these differ by product and why? Evolve a classification system for the soap opera and film material to show how residential backgrounds vary by film type and why. Try to talk with admen, film makers and set designers. Do they have estimates of the effectiveness of their sets for their purposes? Use your best sociological insights to speculate *à la* Handlin on the elements of the sets and why they were put there. Have some products' ads shifted away from the home? If so, why? Your sources are mainly the TV and the movie house, the Late Show and the Late Late Show. Use movie stills, slides, snap shots of the TV, movie strip, book sources.
e) Literatures (1 person)
New Yorker Album of cartoons (or equivalent); child-rearing manuals; legal literatures (zoning, subdivision, building codes, FHA regulations); city planning literatures ('how

to' books for communities, 'standards' literature from APHA, PHA, NRA, ACTION, 'master plans'); folk and pop songs; radio ads; novels; the *words* on the ads. This topic is probably more essay than photo, but it requires classifications, categories and systems for comparison like the others.

In many cartoons (especially in the *New Yorker*) the life-style, through the architecture, interior and exterior, is as brilliantly parodied as the people. Child-rearing manuals deal with the transference of values between generations. What do different manuals (by approach and era) say about the home? 'Ticky-tacky boxes' has passed from song into the language. Are there other songs which comment perhaps less pejoratively on the physical home? What can we learn from the muckrakers? From Jane Austen, Dickens, Scott Fitzgerald, Terry Southern? (Choose your own authors.) From social (not architectural) historians? What types of home selling take place on radio and on what types of stations? What types of verbal pictures are used and how do these compare with their equivalents in newspaper ads?

2 Architects' Attitudes (1 person)
We began our critique of architects' attitudes to housing in the introduction to this studio, suggesting that architects' hearts are in the right place in that they have long been concerned to house the poor; but that their approach has been and still is misdirected in terms of their own goals.

Write an illustrated critique of architectural attitudes to housing and the housing environment from the inception of the Modern Movement to today. This is a reinterpretation of history for a new splinter group of architects – us – whose approach to technology, aesthetics and 'people's values' has diverged strongly, and whose new view encompasses the market and politics – all of which we studied in phase one. Describe traditional Modern approaches to all these aspects of housing using content analysis of the architectural press and not forgetting the writings of architectural historians or Catherine Bauer (*Modern Housing*, 1934).

Discuss the crossing of the Atlantic by CIAM urbanism, its embodiment in US Urban Renewal and what happened. What happened to US architects at the hands of US planners and socially oriented critics? How has this affected architects' attitudes? Discuss the degree to which recent trends – Archigram, Safdie, but also Yelton's 'gentlemen' architects and planners who think they can change the world with their industrialised building systems or a truckload of computer maps (*Connection* 1968-69) – conform to the traditional Modern value system and approach.

3 Sprawl Space and Imagery – Residential Version (3 people)
'This could mean not only are we *not* free from the forms of the past, and from the availability of these forms as typological models, but that,

if we assume we are free, we have lost control over a very active sector of our imaginations and of our power to communicate with others.' (Alan Colquhoun, *Perspecta 12*)

One might add that those who refuse to consider and analyse architecture as form, since form should be a mere resultant of other considerations, tend to find themselves the prisoners of irrelevant formal hand-me-downs whose tyranny is the more severe because it is unconscious.

In this topic formal analysis is used for design research. We aim to: find methods, new and old, of documenting, analysing and interpreting new and emerging residential forms; link these new forms to the architectural tradition by comparing them with older forms; by subjecting them to traditional modes of documentation and criticism – in the way that Warhol put a soupcan in an art gallery – making them part of 'acceptable culture' and usable by architects. We hope thereby to suggest an alternative to the architects' mega-alternatives to urban sprawl. We shall in fact be taking our investigations, started in Las Vegas, into the home.

Consider space, scale, communication, symbol, style, styling. Use analyses, comparisons and images, by photography, collages, diagrams, drawings and schedules.

a) Stylistic Analysis
Split-level-Cape-Cod-ranchers; swinger Versailles; Leisure Worlds; suburbanised-urban; USUR style; architectural heroic. Choose two residential examples of each style and trace their stylistic origins in historical architecture, recent and ancient. In each case use both the neighbourhood and the individual house unit, inside and out. Make a schedule comparing elements of each house and neighbourhood with its exemplars and another comparing the styles with each other by elements.

Choose your elements for comparison to demonstrate how far styling goes; that is, what elements resemble closely their antecedents and where is the past ignored? Where is imagery 'hot' and where 'cool'? Is all the 'hot' imagery related to the style-exemplar? In the bathroom or kitchen or driveway? In the site planning, relation to street, relation to community facilities? Is styling only stuck on facades or does it relate to house plans and location patterns as well? How is styling applied to facades?

b) Space, Scale and Symbol
Symbols in space, scale and space; these seem to be the keys to an understanding of sprawl form and the ways in which it differs from modern and traditional housing forms. Compare the examples from above (and their stylistic antecedents) with: Euro-sprawl, mega-sprawl, primitive and medieval housing, Georgian London and Bath, the New England town, Ville Radieuse, Broadacre City (some of these figure too as stylistic antecedents) and with each other. Use 'symbols in space' and 'scale and space' as categories for comparison. Can you think of others? Comparisons should be at all levels from neighbourhood to interiors.

How much, how and where are symbols used in the examples? What kinds of symbols? How are they perceived at different levels in sprawl space? What different scales, human, vehicle, community and mass, vast and intimate are combined? How is the automobile insinuated in the 'traditional style' examples?

Make diagrammatic plans, sections and elevations, collages, schedules, charts and matrices to make your point.

c) Sprawl Image
Find archetypal and prototypical images, derogatory and sympathetic, for sprawl. Contrast and complement them with opposing or analogous images from other housing. Raid the mass magazines and pop artists as well as the genre painters, scenic or architectural backgrounds in portraits, etc.

Format
Each topic uses content analysis by categories to document and compare the source materials pictorially. Media: movie, slides, collage, drawings, maps, plans and photo-essay. Format: comparative methods of documenting form using charts, schedules, line diagrams and words.

Le Corbusier mixed symbols and words to expound theory, what is the equivalent for our time? Can we propose counter-diagrams where the little houses answer back? What new techniques are required to document new forms? We should aim to dead-pan the material so it speaks for itself. Ruscha has pioneered this treatment in his monographs (*The Sunset Strip, Some Los Angeles Apartments*). It is a way to avoid being upstaged by our own subject matter. It can lead too, toward the methodical rigour which will be required of architectural formal analysis once it is recognised as a legitimate activity.

STUDIO RHA: Phase III: Synthesising
Someone has called Bauhaus education a shotgun marriage of topical preoccupations. This is certainly true of our studio since we have tried to make it a vehicle for several concerns:

1) Social ideals and the desire of young architects to be part of the solution rather than part of the problem.
2) An architectural ontological crisis – what am I?
3) A new pragmatism to fight the old architectural authoritarianism; an openness to others' values, life-styles and attitudes and an interest in popular culture and the existing city, especially slums and suburbs.
4) A revived interest in communication in architecture and therefore in symbolism, eclecticism, style and styling.

These concerns are not necessarily related to each other, except through our interest, now, in them all; and their relation as set out in this studio is not immutable but should alter, as did the Bauhaus pedagogical interfaces, before changing architectural cogencies.

But this next phase, synthesising, should test the validity of our particular shotgun marriage for us today. Do relevant problems come out of the juxtapositions we have made, and does what we have learned help us to deal with them? In the three weeks available we can do no more than begin to think synthetically about the topics we have considered analytically till now.

RESEARCH TOPICS
At least one member of Topic 3 of the last phase and others whose presentation needs completing should work together to finish Phase II so it can be presented in abbreviated form in the final jury. One person should produce a final report to go with the Studio programme, describing what was actually done and giving comments of students and others.

1 Suburban Prototype (2 or 3 people)
If the Suburban Action Institute succeeds there will be a need for low-income suburban housing suitable to the values and life-styles of its occupants on the inside and also suitable not only to its occupants but to their antagonistic neighbours on the outside. This problem of the possible divergence of appearance outside and functional arrangement inside is an ironic one for Modern architects, and the good social reasons behind the split merely increase the irony. Added to it is the problem of maintaining the suburban physical amenities (however defined) while increasing the density.

Borrow a housing programme and site from the Suburban Action Institute or Davidoff's students and suggest, by means of sketch plans, the physical requirements and possibilities of low income housing in suburban areas.

2 Regional Strategy for Low Income Housing (2 or 3 people)
If this country ever grew serious about housing the poor, how might it set about doing so? The Kaiser and Douglas reports each make recommendations over a wide range of possibilities (see the Urban America booklet, *The Ill-Housed*, which summarises and compares their recommendations). We have also come across other sources of strategic ideas on low income housing. How might these and others you can think of be applied in the New Haven metropolitan area given different patterns of resource allocation and different amounts of investment? Propose three or four alternative strategies, some based on the immediate situation without great changes in policies, resource allocation or attitudes and values, and others longer ranged or based on specific policy shifts. This is not a plan; it is a proposed posy of programmes, social, economic, political and physical, with ideas on their interrelation and predictions of their results.

3 New Roles for Architects (1 or 2 people)
In the 1950s and early 1960s, young Ameri-

can architects who saw their best CIAM ideals misused in Urban Renewal, despaired for the 'social housing' which the Modern movement promised, and turned towards city planning as a more powerful occupation than architecture for the achievement of social goals. In planning school they were told by social scientists, a) that architects were responsible for the mess, and b) that what architects did, 'physical planning' as opposed to 'social planning', couldn't do much to alleviate it. Viewing, from within the planning department, the atavistic programmes back there in the architecture department and noting the hostility that was evident when architect friends talked of planning, the architect-planner felt an isolation from both sides.

Since then, things have changed in architecture schools, and a new respect is forming between architects and planners as they meet in advocacy positions; however, many planners (for example Grigsby and Gans) remain sceptical on the social role of architects. Even

such respected sources as *ARse* (#2, 1970) in its taxonomy of latter-day architectural roles is cynical about the usefulness of all of them. Are we? After what we have learned from Phases I and II, does our considered and sympathetic view of architectural social roles still evaluate them as non-existent, impossible and nil? Or are there new ways opening up, there for the finding, in possibly unlikely positions, for innovative architects with a new outlook on housing? What are the alternatives to sitting about and waiting until national priorities alter? Does our new knowledge of attitudes and lifestyles, symbolism and communication in architecture, or housing and marketing techniques suggest anything for our role as socially effective architects?

4 The Oldenburg Interpretation (1 or 2 people)

Do for housing what Oldenburg did for hamburgers. Oldenburg has essentially made us look at hamburgers in another way because he

has portrayed them in an unusual way: big, lacquered and in an art gallery. Does he hate them or love them and should we? Probably he feels some of both, but that doesn't matter – at least, not yet. The first thing is the shift in vision and understanding which an Oldenburg can induce, and the re-interpretation and re-classification of our cultural artifacts which he provides.

Second, in making popular art into high art he legitimises it for the culture vultures. The popular environment, sprawl and strip is drastically in need of a similar service vis-à-vis the Fine Arts Commissions and Sibyl Moholy-Nagy because Pop is unacceptable until it hangs in the academy and only the artist can put it there. Until this happens, hardship will be wrought on people and the environment in the name of good architecture and the fight against 'aesthetic pollution'. And critics will ask why, after all the good intentions, the 'beautified' city should be so dull.

ABOVE: SOUTH PHILADELPHIA AND EXURBAN FACADES; *BELOW*: SOUTH PHILADELPHIA AND EXURBAN INTERIORS

THE HOME

ROBERT VENTURI, STEVEN IZENOUR AND DENISE SCOTT BROWN

The 'Signs of Life: Symbols in the American City' exhibition was an attempt to survey the pluralist aesthetic of the American city and its suburbs, and to understand what the urban landscape means to people, through an analysis of its symbols, their sources and their antecedents. We focused particularly upon the 20th-century commercial strip and suburban sprawl because in these environments the tradition of using symbolism in architecture has continued from the 19th-century city, whereas in areas more directly controlled by architects that tradition was broken by Modern architects' attempts to eradicate historical and symbolic association and decoration from architecture.

Our documentation of sprawl, strip, and city, in the context of one another and of the 19th-century city, was part of a broader effort to understand American architectural tastes and define the role of the architect in relation to them. We contend that:

The rich pervasion of symbols and signs that existed in the historical city continues in the city today, although in a different form.

The 'ordinary' symbols and signs of the commercial and residential environment are not acknowledged but are significant in our daily lives.

In learning to understand our symbols and signs, we come to understand better ourselves and our landscape.

Understanding the *raison d'être* of the physical environment is a necessary prelude to improving it.

A further aim of the exhibition was to suggest to urban designers, architects, and planners, that they open-mindedly study today's urban landscapes, and especially the symbolic meanings people invest in them. In so doing, these urbanists will learn more than they now know about the needs, tastes, and preferences of people whose lives they influence, and particularly about the tastes of groups whose values are different from their own.

The exhibition was structured in three parts: signs and symbols in the home (furnishings, decoration, architectural style and details); on the commercial strip (signs, architecture, gas stations, motels, etc); and on the street (urban commercial streets, civic buildings as symbols, parks, squares, etc).

The introduction to the show outlines the kind of issues it raised:

What makes a house look like a house, a school like a school, or a bank like a bank?

What makes a gasoline station look like a good neighbour? This exhibition is intended to show that the forms of architecture have symbolic meaning and give messages about the environment that make it comprehensible and therefore usable by people in their daily lives.

For example, the flashing electric sign on Route 66 tells us specifically, EAT HERE, and its design may suggest the kind of eating available, perhaps family dining, soft-light off the main highway. Suburbia's curving roads and tended lawns, its pitch-roofed houses, colonial doorways, and shuttered windows tell us, without need of signs, that here is a community that values tradition, pride of ownership, and rural life.

The Home section surveyed suburban and urban residential neighbourhoods and individual houses. It focused particularly upon the decorations people add to their houses and yards once they occupy them. But it surveyed, too, developer house styles and the housing content of television commercials, home journals, automobile advertisements, *New Yorker* cartoons, developers' blurbs, and mail-order catalogues, because these mass media sources attempt to reach their markets by using residential symbols that reflect current social and personal aspirations.

The following are excerpts from the text of the Home section:

The physical elements of suburbia – the roads, houses, roofs, lawns, and front doors – serve practical purposes such as giving access and shelter, but they also serve as means of self-expression for suburban residents.

Winding roads, romantic rooflines, garden ornaments, Colonial front doors and coach lanterns are decorative elements with symbolic overtones that residents use to communicate with others about themselves. The communication is mainly about social status, social aspirations, personal identity, individual freedom, and nostalgia for another time or place. The symbolic subject matter of residential decoration comes from history, rural life, patriotism, and the estates of the rich.

Inexpensive land helped people move to the suburbs. Financial, banking, and government agencies favoured suburban development. Today, increased costs have forced suburbanites to consider housing that is denser and more urban than the traditional detached suburban home. Multi-family housing forms, – garden apartments, 'town houses', patio houses, and quadroplexes – appear with increasing frequency, often in planned communities. Mobile homes are popular. Each residential type appears to suit a specific market – singles, young married couples, young families, and retired people. Multi-family types frequently adopt New England or European small town imagery, whereas mobile homes imitate the one-family, detached house.

A house is an extension of one's own physical being. It has come to stand for privacy, mastery, self-expression, self-esteem, identity, and security. It is the stage set for playing out one's life. Homeowners express their personal identities and social aspirations through the symbols they apply to their homes. Symbols are borrowed from American history, rural life, the patriotic tradition, and the estates of the rich.

'Suburban sprawl' eludes our concepts of urban form. It isn't enclosed or directed like the space of traditional cities – it is open and indeterminate. In the undefined space of the commercial strip, we find our way through signs and symbols, and in the vast space of suburbia there is a similar need for explicit symbolism. Some physical elements of suburbia, for example, roads, roofs, and doorways, fulfil functional requirements and are bearers of symbolic messages as well. Together with the more explicitly symbolic facade decorations and front yard ornaments, these elements help to define suburban space, using their symbolic content to make up for their relatively small size. The different elements of suburban space communicate their symbolic messages at different scales, depending on the distance from which they are read.

The eclectic ornament on and around the relatively small house acts as a visual booster between the house and the curb, reaching out to you across the big lawn, linking the symbolic architecture to the moving vehicle. The decorated house and lawn make an impact that pure architectural articulation could never make, at least in time, before you have passed on to the next house.

The front facade is the surface on which the builder applies the most elaborate elements of styling. Residents embellish it with shutters, ornamental carriage lamps, screen doors, personal messages, and seasonal decorations, and with the most ubiquitous of all decorations, the American flag and eagle. Residences with stylish fronts and plain backs, 'Queen Anne in front and Mary Anne behind', are so common that they offer the media a constant source of comment.

In most houses, the sequence from entry, through living spaces, to bedroom areas is also a sequence from public to private. This is particularly true of the 19th- and early 20th-century house where uses of rooms were more specifically defined than they are today and where there was a gradation of symbolism from communal to personal. For example, ancestral portraits were in the living or dining room, trophies and personal mementos in the study, and family photographs in the bedroom.

Today's recombinations of rooms sometimes spell a change in the type of imagery. A den or a family room is a living area with personal rather than public imagery; the kitchen in the kitchen-dining-living space may have cabinets that don't look too different from the cabinets that house the family TV set.

One caveat: suburban housing symbolism doesn't tell us why people live in suburbs, nor does it reveal much about the problems they experience in suburbia; it merely indicates some of their aspirations while they are there.

The same applies to urban housing. Also, although the mass media provide interesting information on some group attitudes towards housing, this source should not be taken as the last word on personal and social values in the United States. However, Americans' self-expression in and around their homes is an important clue to their attitudes, the more so because this form of self-expression is practised by almost all social groups, by young and old, rich and poor, renters and owners, urbanites and suburbanites.

ABOVE: LEVITTOWN; *OVERLEAF*: THEMES AND IDEALS OF THE AMERICAN SUBURB

MERICAN SUBURB

he rural life
gia for an
ressures behind
conomic forces

and developments in household appliances and leisure
equipment, bear universally upon suburbanites and
are reflected in their houses, as well as in developers' advertising and the mass media.

ECONOMICS

People still want to move to the suburbs, though
country life exists there only in symbols. '

PERSONAL & SOCIAL IDENTITY

"To own one's own home is a physical expression of individualis
of enterprise, of independence, and of freedom of spirit."
(Herbert Hoover 1931)

A house is the largest single purchase most families make in their lifet

The suburban house borrows symbols from the estate.

assumed aspirations of its potential buyers.

"A man's house is his castle."

AT THE DOORSTEP

ouse front is treated as a kind of billboard
h residents and builders.

ol of hospitality and warmth, the front door
e first element for symbolic decoration.

ntial building materials are symbolic, too.

IN THE BACKYARD

The suburban backyard and patio afford an area for informal out-
door living and contain the barbeque, swing, pool and tool shed.

The rear facade supports less symbolic imagery than does the front.

IN BETWEEN

The side yard is neither private enough for family use nor public
enough for symbolic communication.

IN THE HOUSE

"Down home comfort and right nice styling...." (Tennessee Ernie Ford for Comfort-Mates)

In most houses, the sequence from entry, through living spaces,
to bedroom areas is also a sequence from public to private.

Traditionally, the fire place, the hearth, has been the great
symbol for home and almost synonymous with it.

PREVIOUS PAGE: SUBURBAN SPACE, SCALE AND SYMBOL; *ABOVE AND BELOW*: SIMILAR HOUSES PERSONALISED OVER TIME, AND THE BUNGALOW

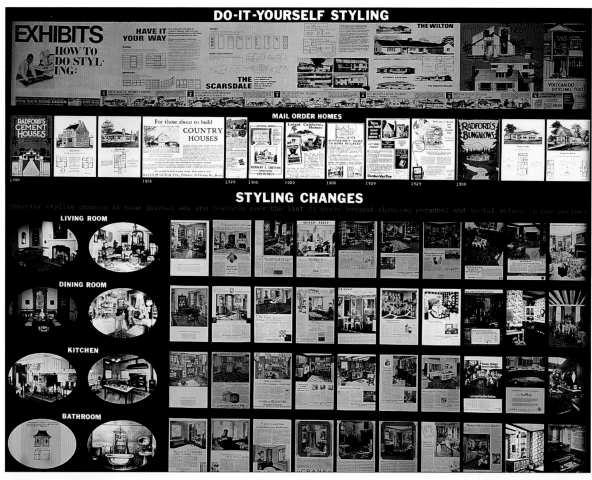

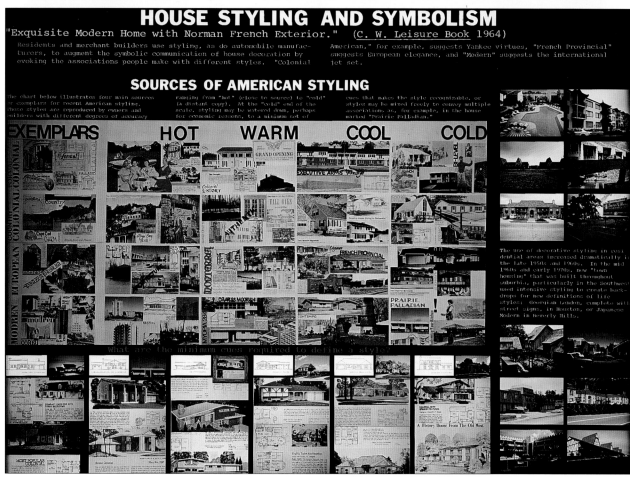

ABOVE AND BELOW: HOUSE-STYLING AND SYMBOLISM

EN · LUTYENS · LE CORBUSIER · TOSCANINI · LOO

VENTURI HOUSE, WISSAHICKON AVENUE, 1972 TO PRESENT
PHILADELPHIA, PENNSYLVANIA

This Art Nouveau house was designed by Milton Medary in 1909. In addition to being the Venturis' home, the house has served as a laboratory for investigations into the use of decoration to enrich interior surfaces. The interiors are complex in their mixture of furnishings, patterns and colours; they play around the symbolic idea of home, and the representation of home that people understand and feel comfortable with; and they confront the issue of taste and the variety of taste cultures that are represented in the notion of home. Despite the varied styles of the decoration and furnishings, everything hangs together; the blending of periods and styles seems natural for a home that has been lived in by a family over the years.

OPPOSITE: CLOSE-UP OF PATTERNING IN DINING-ROOM; *ABOVE AND BELOW*: DINING AND LIVING-ROOMS

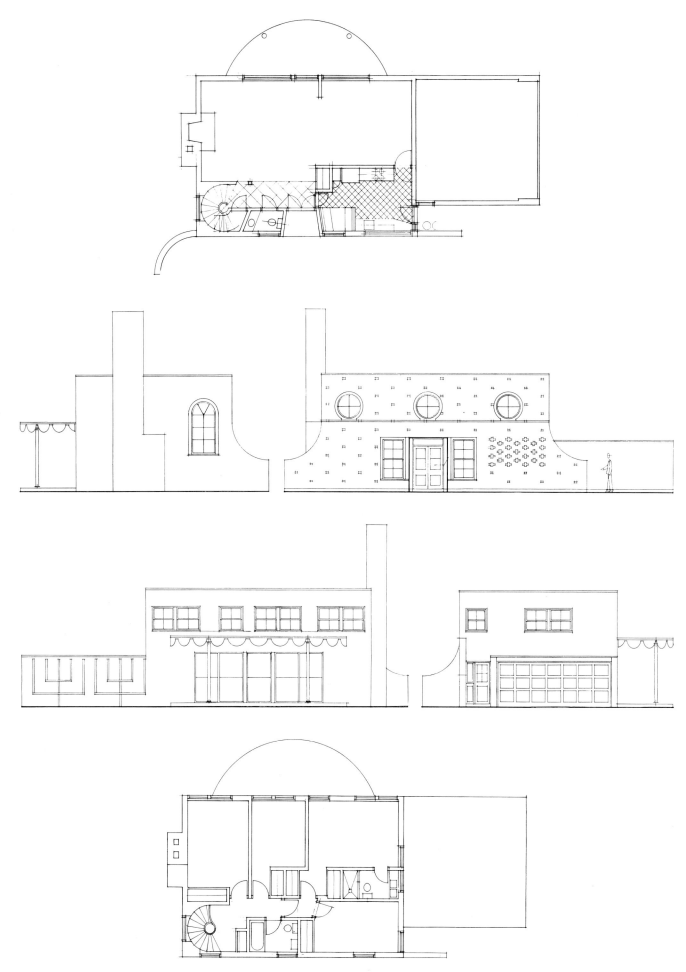

FROM ABOVE: GROUND-FLOOR PLAN; SIDE ELEVATION TOWARDS WISSAHICKON AVE AND FRONT ELEVATION; REAR ELEVATION AND
SIDE ELEVATION TOWARDS GARAGE COURT; FIRST-FLOOR PLAN

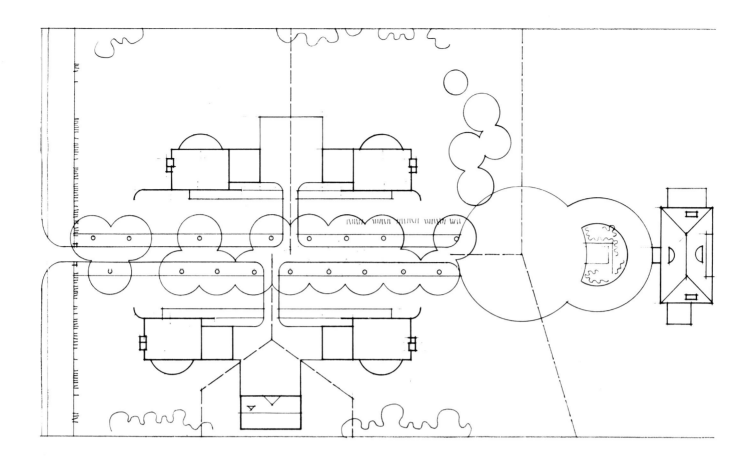

WISSAHICKON AVENUE HOUSING, PROJECT, 1972
PHILADELPHIA, PENNSYLVANIA

A large, old, five-acre estate in West Mount Airy, Philadelphia, was to be subdivided, the rear portion sold with the original house, and sites along the driveway leading to it sold off in six lots. We produced a design to show the West Mount Airy civic association, that the subdivision could be done well. We developed a series of 'manorettes' – designed to go with the Art Nouveau old house, and in a way to lead up to it. The small houses would have their own character, yet be in keeping with their larger neighbours. We felt we could achieve this through the way they related to each other, rather than through size, which wasn't an option.

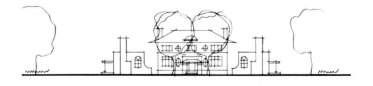

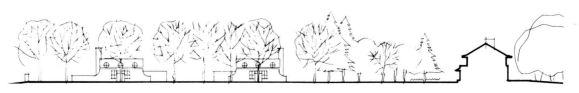

ABOVE: SITE PLAN; *MIDDLE*: CROSS SECTION OF SITE; *BELOW*: LONG SECTION OF SITE

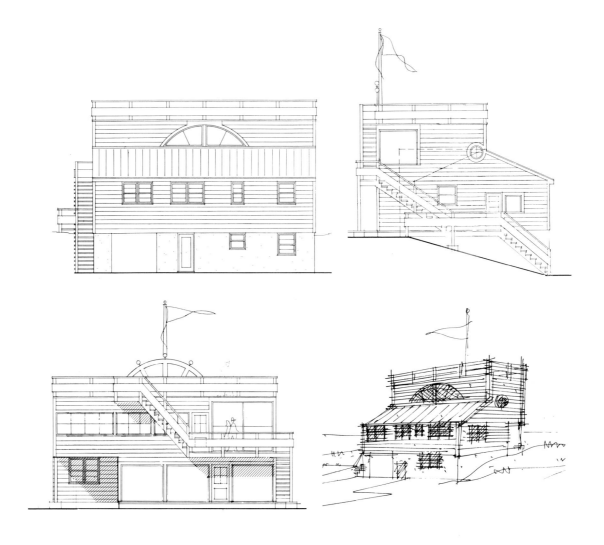

ADDITION TO HOUSE IN SEA ISLE CITY, 1972
SEA ISLE CITY, NEW JERSEY

An extension to a seaside bungalow at the New Jersey shore. On the land side, the plan and roofline of the original house are left undisturbed. Facing the ocean, a second storey is added. It maintains the construction systems of the bungalow below but superimposes minimal, though visible, nautical allusions.

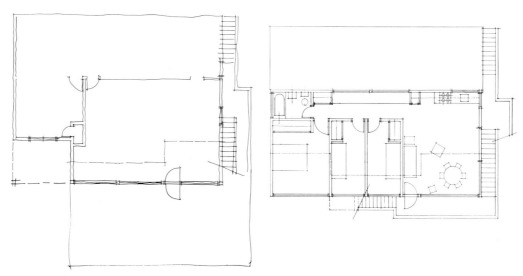

ABOVE: FRONT AND SIDE ELEVATIONS; *MIDDLE*: OCEAN ELEVATION AND SKETCH; *BELOW*: GROUND AND FIRST-FLOOR PLANS

TUCKER HOUSE, 1974
WESTCHESTER COUNTY, NEW YORK

At the time this house was commissioned, the client wanted quarters only for himself. From this simple programme evolved a tribute both to the plain American shingled house and to the tradition of Mannerist gesture. It is a house designed to look ordinary at first glance, but to be extraordinary at second glance and while living in it. This is a small house with big scale: its few parts are big and its form is simple, bold and symmetrical. Recessive in colour and shingle-texture, sitting among the trees on its lush, semi-rural site, this building is a tall, wooden object. The facade appears to be dominated by a gable although, in fact, a pitched roof rises steeply to a central point. There is a wide overhang on all four sides and windows in the shingled walls are placed only to reflect interior demands. The entry level is devoted to practical spaces – a hall which doubles as a dining area, a kitchen, a bedroom, and a bathroom arranged to serve both the bedroom and the public spaces. A staircase, wider at the bottom, rises against one wall of the house, turning at the top to open into the extraordinary major living space above. It is at once grand and intimate, formal and relaxed. Three walls have large windows and the fourth, the staircase wall, is dominated by a large hearth. The fireplace structure echoes the shape of the house. A narrow staircase rises above the living-room to a balcony with booklined walls and a window-seat reading nook, that looks out over the living-room, through a large oval window, into the surrounding woods.

ABOVE: FRONT VIEW; *BELOW*: STUDIES OF SECTION AND FRONT ELEVATIONS WITH AND WITHOUT ROOF

OPPOSITE: SECOND-FLOOR LANDING; *ABOVE*: FRONT, SIDE AND REAR ELEVATIONS; *MIDDLE*: LIVING-ROOM; *BELOW*: GROUND-FLOOR PLAN, SECTION AND FIRST-FLOOR PLAN

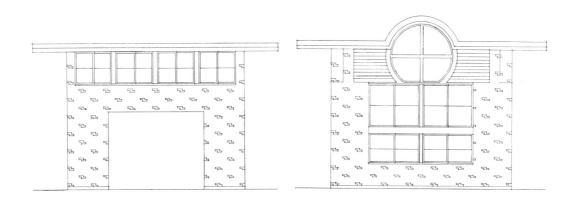

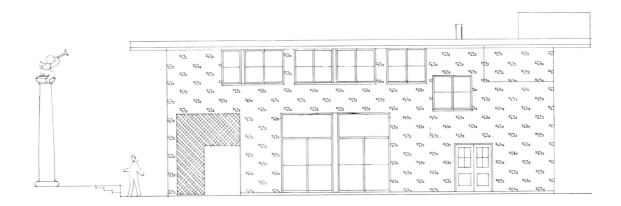

DREAM HOUSE, PROJECT, 1974
JERSEY SHORE, PENNSYLVANIA

A simple vacation house in the tradition of the Lieb House with one large living space and kitchen on the ground floor, and four bunk-bedrooms on the second floor. The exterior is a flat-roofed box with applied brick ornament.

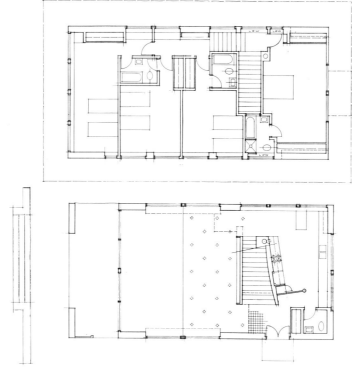

FROM ABOVE: REAR ELEVATION AND FRONT ELEVATION; SIDE ELEVATION; FIRST-FLOOR PLAN; GROUND-FLOOR PLAN

HOUSE IN BERMUDA, 1975
TUCKERS TOWN, BERMUDA

This summer vacation house is sited on a cliff dropping to a beach. Its design responds to local guide-lines requiring use of traditional styles and materials. The house is divided into three abutting pavilions: service areas and kitchen; master suite, dining room, and other sleeping rooms; and living-room. The narrowness of the pavilions allows for good cross ventilation, which is crucial for comfort in this tropical climate. The gabled tile roofs are used to collect rainwater – a local necessity. On entering the house, the sea view is dramatically exaggerated by the view down the main stairs to the beach and the bay beyond.

ABOVE: FRONT VIEW; *BELOW*: DINING-ROOM

ABOVE: SIDE VIEW; *MIDDLE*: EXTENDED SIDE ELEVATION; *BELOW*: VIEW FROM VERANDAH

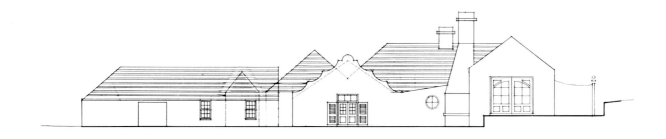

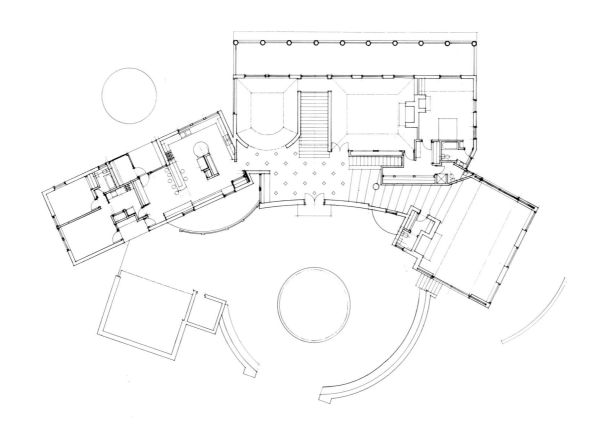

ABOVE: EXTENDED FRONT ELEVATION; *MIDDLE*: GROUND-FLOOR PLAN; *BELOW*: EXTENDED REAR ELEVATION

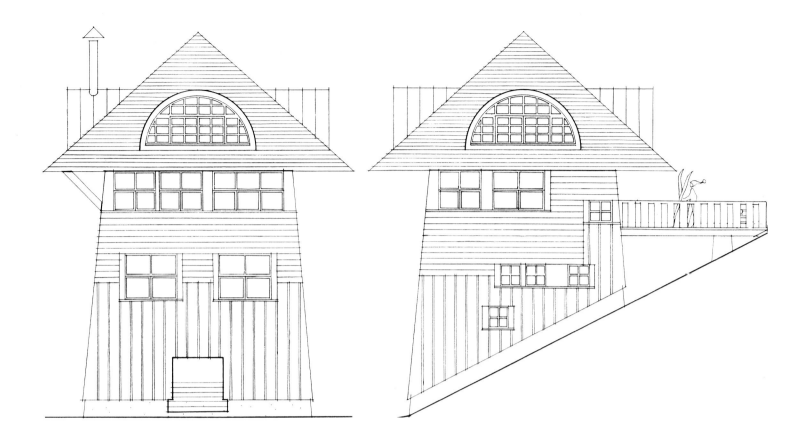

HOUSE IN VAIL, 1975
VAIL, COLORADO

This Ski House is on the steep northern slope of the mountain above Vail in a stand of aspen trees and evergreen bushes. It was designed for a young family with two children and their friends and was to accommodate a large number of guests.

The building is a four-storey tower at home among the tall, straight trees. The ground floor contains storage, laundry and a sauna. The first, bedrooms and small bunkrooms for guests. The second, the kitchen and dining spaces with a separate room to be used as a play, TV and guest room. The third floor, in the tree tops, has big dormer windows with deep window seats that can serve as additional beds. The flooring is wide pine planks; there is cedar siding inside and out and the house is furnished with a collection of Gustav Stickley Mission oak furniture.

OPPOSITE: FRONT VIEW; *ABOVE*: FRONT AND SIDE ELEVATIONS; *BELOW*: ILLUSTRATION OF EXTERIOR

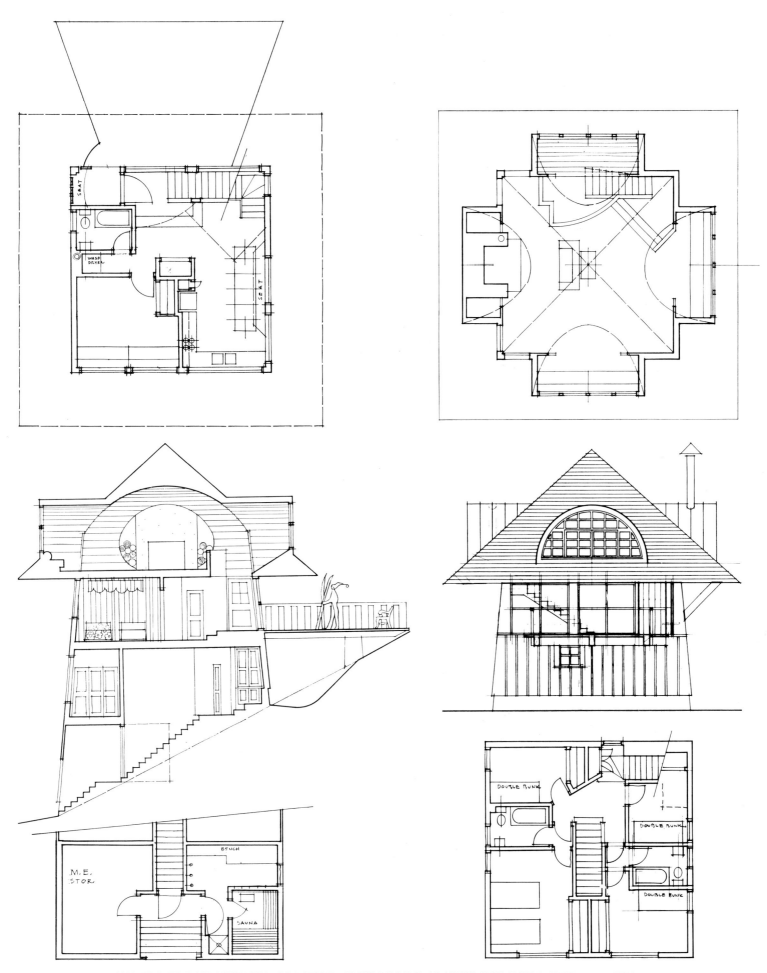

OPPOSITE: THIRD-FLOOR GUEST ROOM; *ABOVE*: SECOND AND THIRD-FLOOR PLANS; *MIDDLE*: CROSS SECTION AND REAR ELEVATION;
BELOW: GROUND AND FIRST-FLOOR PLANS

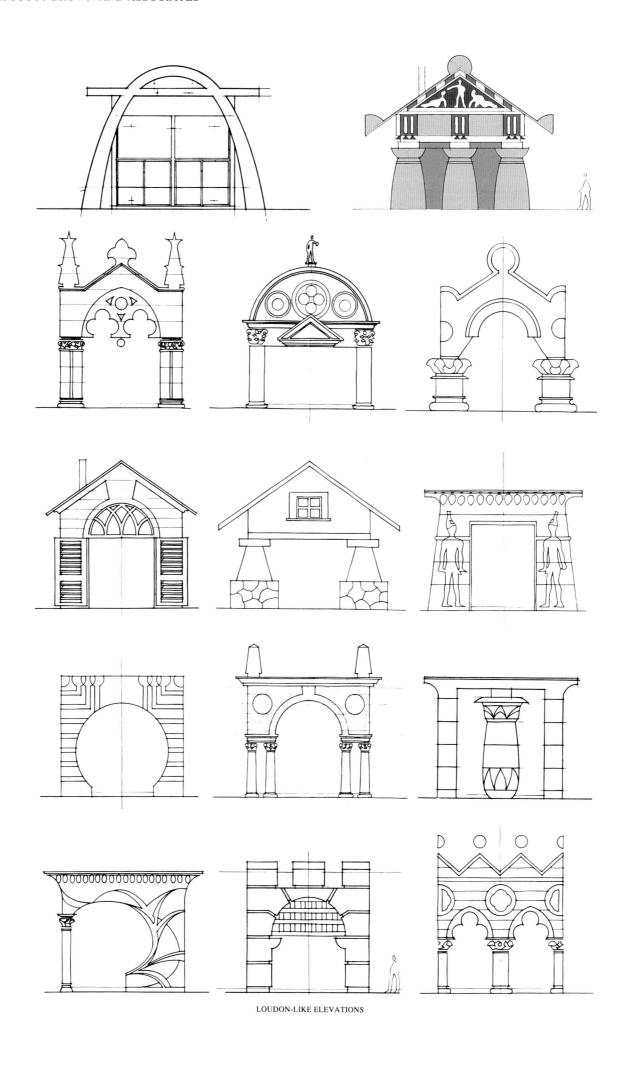

LOUDON-LIKE ELEVATIONS

ECLECTIC HOUSE, PROJECT, 1977

An imaginary, minimal vacation house serves as a point of departure for a theoretical exercise on the idea of the decorated front and the ordinary behind. The house series is a homage to Loudon and a response to the analyses of 'Learning from Levittown'. In it, style and function are juxtaposed, not distorted; and styles are applied to the front, while plan, section and the other three elevations remain constant.

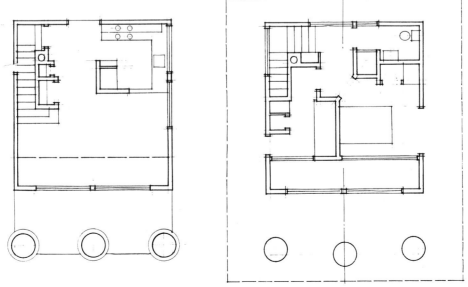

ABOVE: CROSS SECTION AND REAR ELEVATION; *MIDDLE*: FRONT AND SIDE ELEVATIONS; *BELOW*: GROUND AND FIRST-FLOOR PLANS

HOUSE ON LONG ISLAND I, PROJECT, 1977
LONG ISLAND, NEW YORK

This vacation cottage is designed around a barrel-vaulted living-room that houses the owner's painting collection. The style is simple in the bungalow tradition, with a gabled end, a hip roof and dormers.

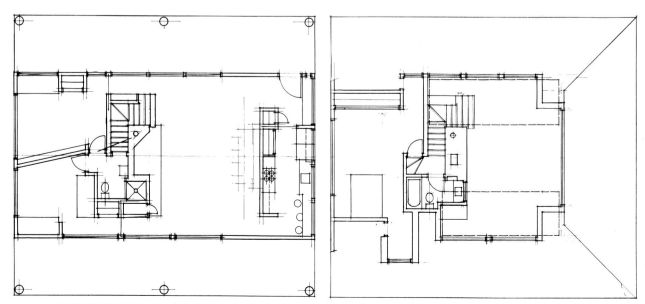

ABOVE: CROSS SECTION AND REAR ELEVATION; *MIDDLE*: LONG SECTION AND SIDE ELEVATION; *BELOW*: GROUND AND FIRST-FLOOR PLANS

HOUSE IN ABSECON, PROJECT, 1977
ABSECON, NEW JERSEY

This is an all year round house at the shore. The plan is a simple rectangular box with one large living space on the ground floor and two bedrooms and a study on the first floor. The dining area is defined by corner piers and a two-storey vault. The exterior is a flat-roofed clapboard box with applied wood ornament representing a formal French Neo-classicism executed in the American Carpenter tradition.

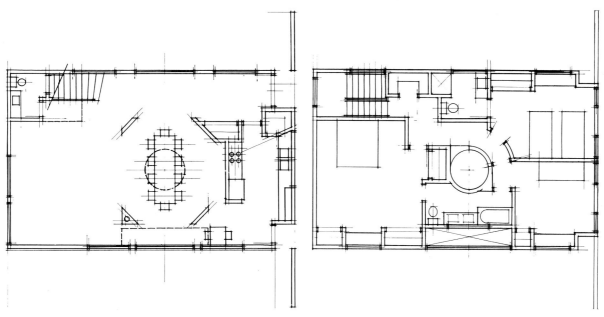

ABOVE: FRONT AND REAR ELEVATIONS; *MIDDLE*: SIDE ELEVATIONS; *BELOW*: GROUND AND FIRST-FLOOR PLANS

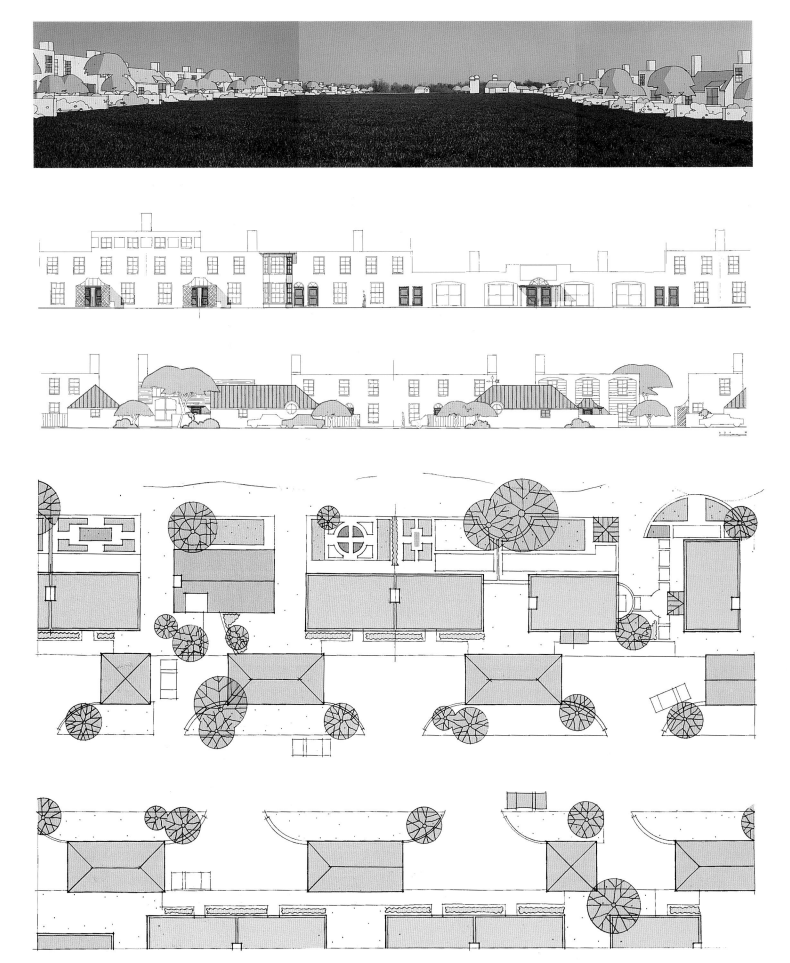

FROM ABOVE: PERSPECTIVAL VIEW; ELEVATION OF TOWNHOUSES AND CONDOMINIUMS; PARTIAL ELEVATION OF HOUSES ALONG CURVED STREET; PLAN OF HOUSES ALONG CURVED STREETS

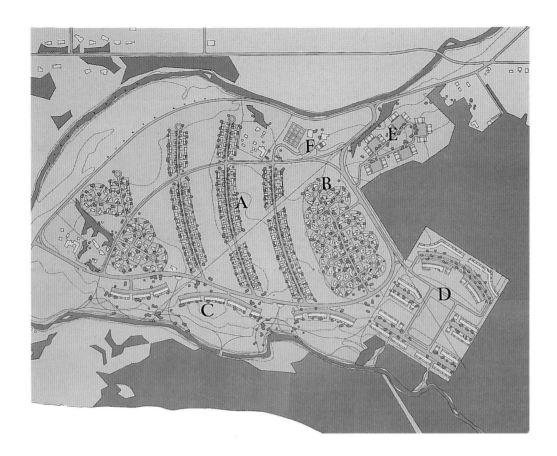

PRINCETON HOUSING, PROJECT, 1978
PRINCETON, NEW JERSEY

We approached the design of a 1,000-unit housing development on a 600-acre site adjacent to the Institute for Advanced Study with a primary concern for the retention of the quality of the beautiful existing rural landscape.

The development programme called for single family detached and semi-detached houses, townhouses, and duplexes. Several housing groupings were evolved to correspond with the variety of settings offered by the site: open fields, an enclosed clearing in the woods that resembled a formal garden, and an ecologically valu-able lowland of stream, marsh, and flood plain.

The design is intended to suggest the Regency and Greek Revival buildings in the area that are valued by many Princetonians. It is an architecture of white walls, flat roofs, bays and sash windows. Although it is rural, it is not rustic. Its character is one of unified diversity. In these settings, housing clusters around cul-de-sacs, borders along the fields in linear ribbons, meanders along the valley in loose linear groupings, or sits formally around commons within the formal garden and at the edge of the main road.

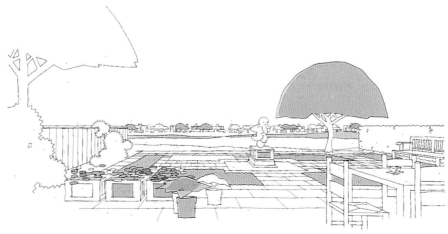

ABOVE: SITE PLAN; *BELOW*: VIEW FROM A HOUSE AT THE EDGE OF THE FIELD

ABOVE: REAR VIEW; *BELOW*: FRONT VIEW; *FACING PAGE*: SITE PLAN

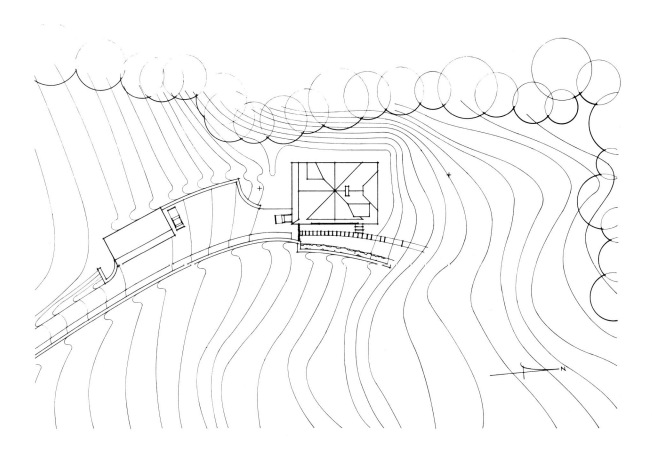

HOUSE IN DELAWARE, 1978
NEW CASTLE COUNTY, DELAWARE

This house for a family of three has an unusual programme. The wife, a musician, required a music room appropriate for small gatherings, and containing an organ, two pianos, and a harpsichord. The family wanted big windows facing the woods for bird-watching and the husband needed a study in a remote part of the house.

The house sits in rolling fields at the edge of a valley to the west and woods to the north. Eighteenth-century Classical barns with generous scale and low horizontal proportions are traditional in northern Delaware where the site is located. The walls of these barns are field stone with wood frame and siding in some upper sections. We based the form and symbolism of the house on this indigenous architecture, to make it look at home in its rural setting and to conform to the easy, generous, yet unpretentious way of living our clients envisioned. The landscaping is cultivated in the immediate vicinity
of the house, but natural beyond.

Vincent Scully described the evocative simplicity of this house in Architectural Digest, *March 1985:*

'Reference is more or less to the Shingle Style and its American Colonial detailing, but more directly to the Shingle Style's English wing and to the 'sweetness and light' of Queen Anne. Finally, it is Kate Greenaway's rose-covered cottage that comes to life before us, right out of a child's book. It evokes an unparalleled domestic innocence and peace in an atmosphere of middle-class goodness of pre-World War I vintage. The open arch plays a considerable part in setting this stage. It is pure fantasy, but it also screens the big windows of the gable so that they cannot compete with the range of smaller windows below them, out of which the arch itself seems to rise like a trellis for roses. The whole respires with the airs of a garden. It is a dollhouse at the foot of the slope.'

ABOVE: VIEW OF HOUSE IN LANDSCAPE; *BELOW*: DINING AREA

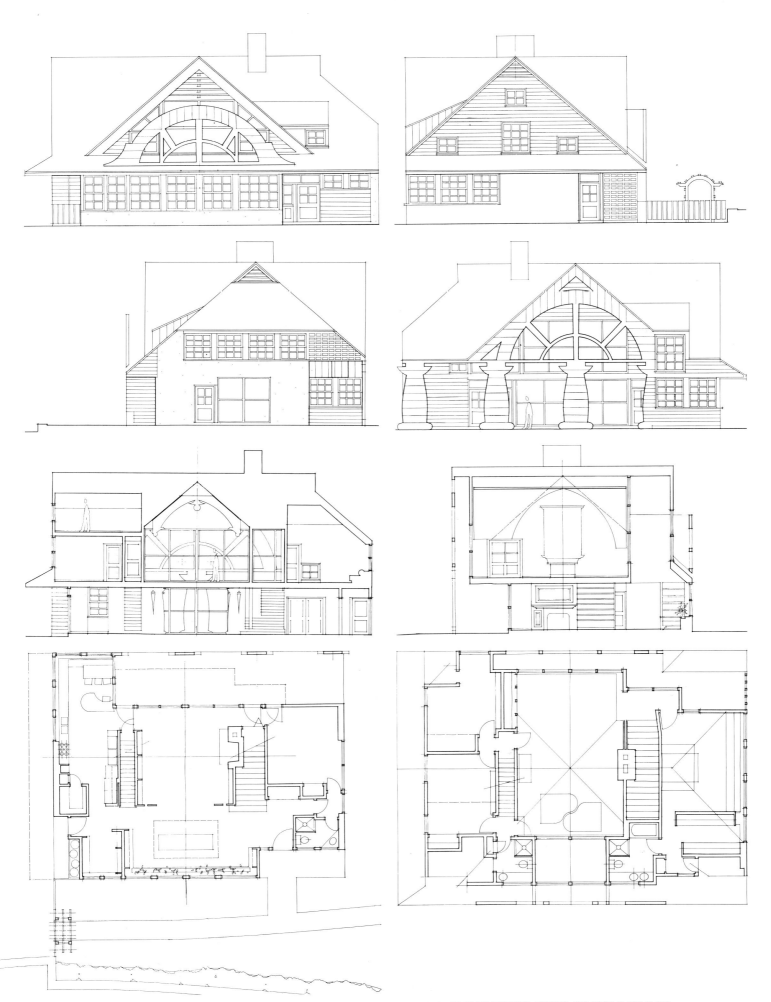

FROM ABOVE: EAST AND SOUTH ELEVATIONS; NORTH AND WEST ELEVATIONS; LONG AND CROSS SECTIONS; GROUND AND FIRST-FLOOR PLANS

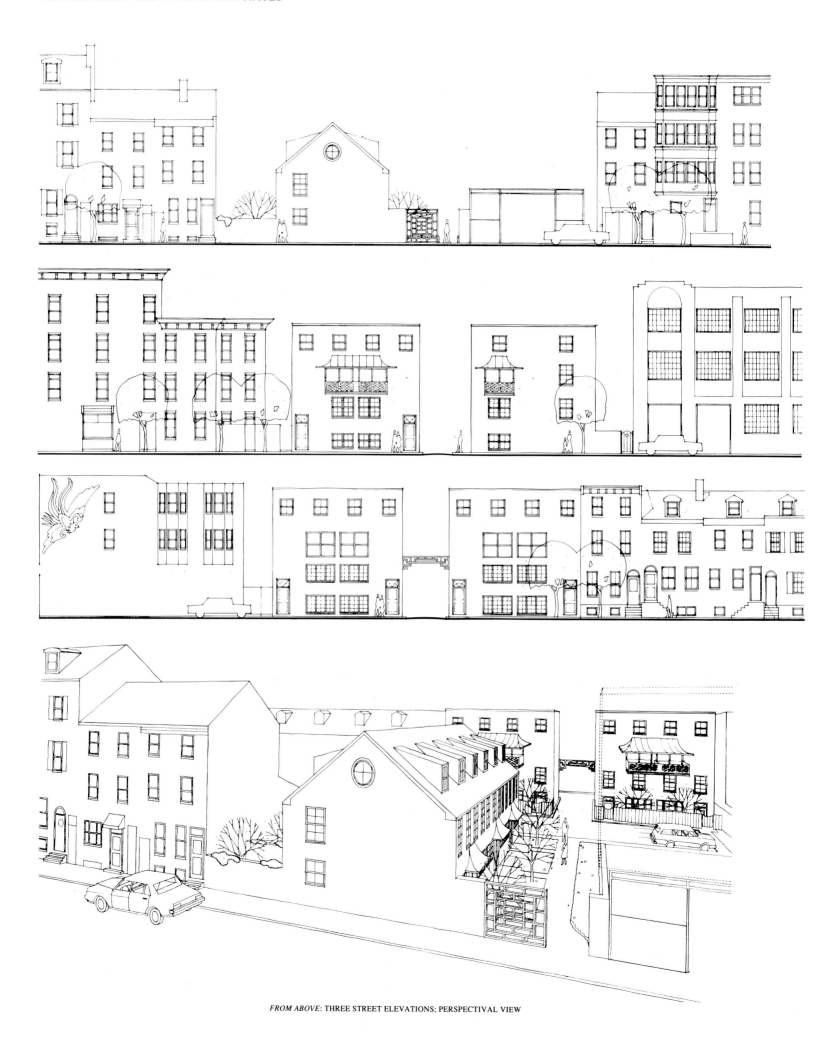

FROM ABOVE: THREE STREET ELEVATIONS; PERSPECTIVAL VIEW

CHINATOWN HOUSING, 1979
PHILADELPHIA, PENNSYLVANIA

The project consists of 25 dwelling units constructed on land made available by the Philadelphia Redevelopment Authority. The project includes 13 rowhouse units, with three and four bedrooms, for sale to middle income purchasers at market rates, and 12 duplex condominium units for sale to qualified low income purchasers through the Federal Assistance Program. The project occupies two sites and includes interior parking courts and landscaped areas.

The character of the architecture is modelled on Philadelphia prototypes. The rowhouse units have sloping roofs, dormers and entrance hoods following traditional design. The duplex units, which are located along the perimeter of the site facing streets with higher traffic densities, have flat roofs and provide gardens for the lower units and balconies for the upper units. The balconies have hoods and railings whose design is derived from Georgian Chippendale precedent. The houses have generous windows and there is protected offstreet pedestrian circulation.

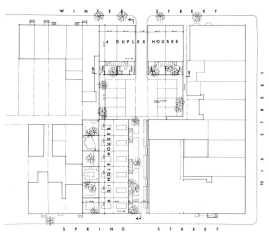

ABOVE: EXTERIOR VIEW; *BELOW*: SITE PLAN

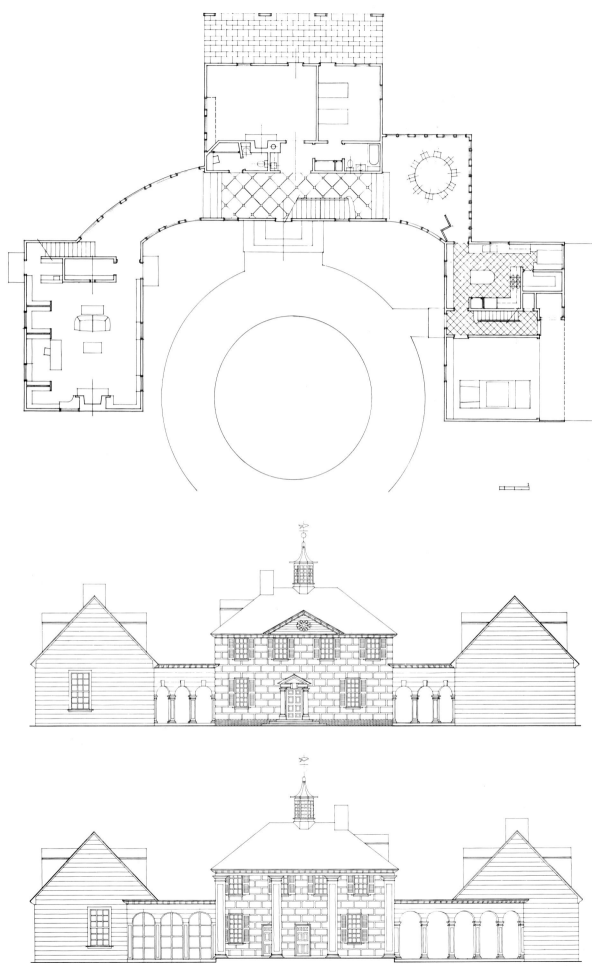

ABOVE: GROUND-FLOOR PLAN; *MIDDLE*: FRONT ELEVATION; *BELOW*: REAR ELEVATION

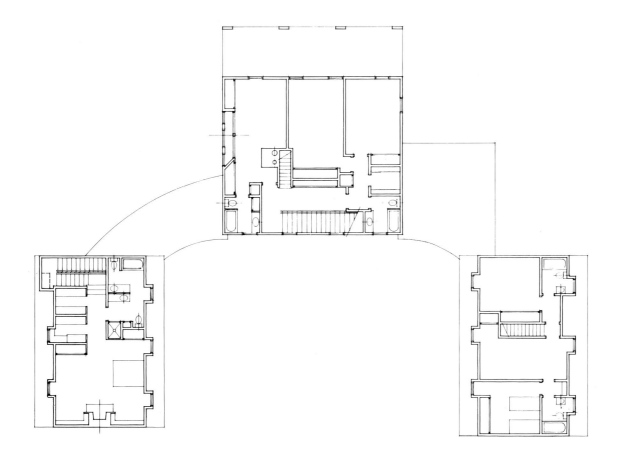

'MOUNT VERNON' HOUSE, PROJECT, 1979

This was a preliminary design for a house on a big rural site for a family that requested it look like Mount Vernon, to suit their country way of life as well for their American antique furniture. Its plan accommodated these and other particular requirements of the programme such as extra garages and facilities connected with maintenance of the estate.

For Americans Mount Vernon, as the home of George Washington, is so highly charged with symbolism that it is hard to see the building as form as well as symbol; that is, to balance form and symbol in the way one

usually does in the perception of a work of art. We have purposely made the building not too correct as one can't – and shouldn't – be totally accurate historically.

In our Mount Vernon some of the proportions are off – the length of the main block is short; the scale changes – the side wings are relatively big in scale, for instance; the detailing is simplified, flattened, and therefore generalised. All of these modifications accommodate modern requirements of the programme and exaggerate its symbolic content. Taking something familiar and making it slightly off can make its familiarity eloquent.

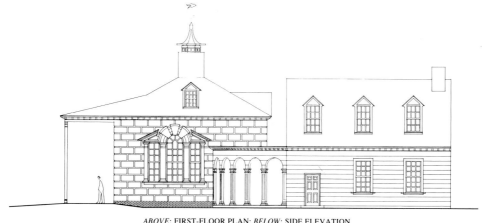

ABOVE: FIRST-FLOOR PLAN; *BELOW*: SIDE ELEVATION

ABOVE AND BELOW: FRONT AND REAR VIEWS; *FACING PAGE*: FRONT VIEW OF HOUSE AND STUDIO

COXE-HAYDEN HOUSE AND STUDIO, 1979
BLOCK ISLAND, RHODE ISLAND

The site for these two big-little buildings is an open meadow running down to a salt water pond on Block Island. The large building has living, dining and kitchen areas on the ground floor, bedroom and bath on the first floor, and a writing studio above in the gable. The smaller building has a garage-workshop below, with two guest rooms and a bath above.

The stylistic source is the countrified Classical Revival bungalow typical of many 19th-century buildings on Block Island. Unlike the New England salt box tradition of small windows, asymmetrical gables, and small scale details, this style had a 'Temple' front with symmetrical entrance, a simple profile and over-scaled overhangs, windows, battenboards and trim.

The resulting studio and guest house are an expression of complex simplicity, new oldness, and the blending of individual expression with an established architectural vocabulary. Their combination of ordinary historical images and associations with big scale elements creates an extraordinary monumental presence that belies their small size.

Great attention was paid to getting the 'right' view, the 'right' entrance, the 'right' feel as specified by the client in an informally written, seven-page programme. For example, the windows are grouped to provide the light and particular views requested inside the three-storey house, but from the outside their design and placement seem to indicate a two-storey house in keeping with its particular place and community. The interior details, such as the cupboard on the first-floor landing and the kitchen cabinet edging, contribute to the client's desire for 'stimulating spaces' without sacrificing the request for simplicity and ease of use.

The house received a 'Record Houses' Award in 1982, and an AIA National Honour Award in 1983.

One critic said: 'the house and studio are a homage to the beach cottages of memory. Indeed, they are not a copy of any old buildings, but a distillation of their elements with contemporary modifications. The buildings seem not so much imitations, but memories themselves.'

ABOVE AND BELOW: INTERIOR VIEWS

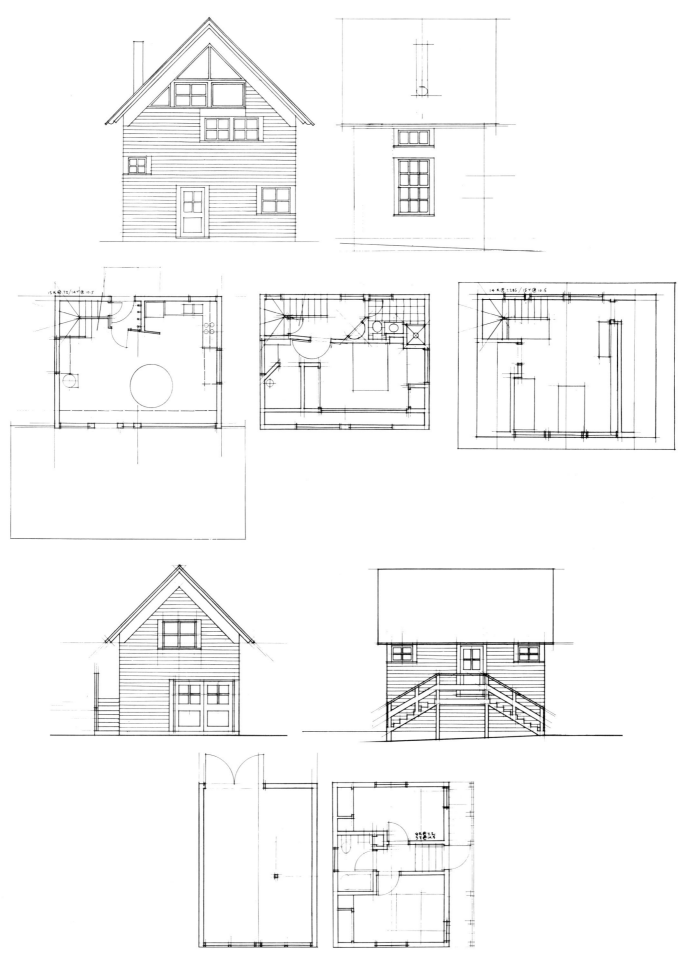

FROM ABOVE: FRONT AND SIDE ELEVATIONS OF HOUSE; GROUND, FIRST AND SECOND-FLOOR PLANS OF HOUSE;
FRONT AND SIDE ELEVATIONS OF STUDIO; GROUND AND FIRST-FLOOR PLANS OF STUDIO

HOUSE ON NANTUCKET ISLAND, 1981
NANTUCKET ISLAND, MASSACHUSETTS

This is a small vacation house overlooking the sea. The major living spaces are located on the first floor for a view of the water. Sleeping areas are on the ground and second floor. The prostyle form of the building with its long sides perpendicular to the shore allows each room to view the water. The narrow front of the house incorporates porches on two levels. The living/dining area opens onto its porch with a series of glass doors and windows, creating a transparent wall that is framed by the tracery of the outer wall.

The house is sheathed with the wood shingles and masonry of traditional Nantucket houses. Windows, doors and trim are also derived from earlier models, yet their proportions and placement on the facades accommodate the modern form and programme of the house.

This house was not built as shown here; its design was modified by the design review process of the Nantucket Historical Commission.

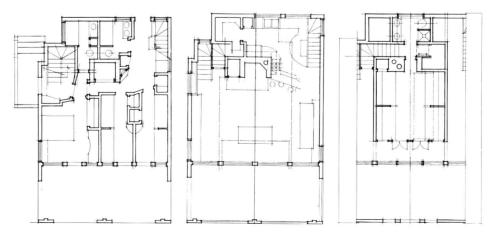

ABOVE: FRONT ELEVATION AND SECTION; *MIDDLE*: SIDE AND REAR ELEVATIONS; *BELOW*: GROUND, FIRST AND SECOND-FLOOR PLANS

HOUSE ON LONG ISLAND II, PROJECT, 1981
EAST HAMPTON, NEW YORK

A summer house facing the ocean and recalling a shingle house of the 1880s. Its composition starts out symmetrical but evolves asymmetrically towards its perimeters to accommodate specific requirements of its plan. It contains an aerie-attic study.

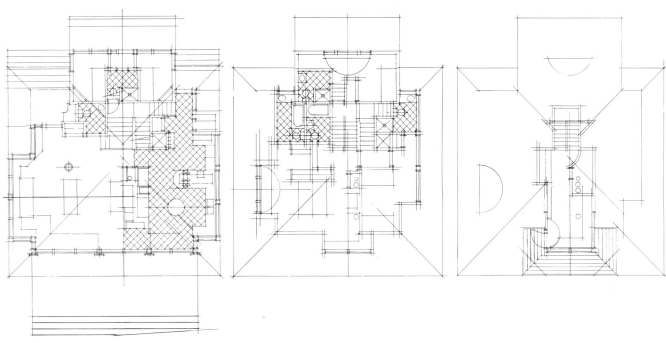

ABOVE: WEST AND NORTH ELEVATIONS; *MIDDLE*: CONTEXT ELEVATION; *BELOW*: GROUND, FIRST AND SECOND-FLOOR PLANS

ABOVE AND BELOW: VIEWS OF THE REAR AND FRONT OF THE HOUSE

HOUSE ON LONG ISLAND III, 1982
EAST HAMPTON, NEW YORK

The clients wanted a year-round weekend retreat that would exploit the beauty of their wooded site (fronting a salt pond behind ocean dunes) and reflect the dignified turn-of-the-century houses nearby. They wanted the house to be practical for two in the winter yet accommodate the family and guests in the summer.

The house is a rectangular structure of shingle and clapboard with a gambrel roof, evoking three centuries of houses and barns in the region. Two main rooms occupy the lower floor. A large living space opens onto full-length porches, front and back. The kitchen also opens on to both porches. Thus, the main floor can expand into an open pavilion or contract to become a warm refuge in winter.

An office and three bedrooms are upstairs. A pool house-boat-cum-house-garage faces the main house. The lawn is enclosed by native trees, shrubs and meadow plants. In a place where storms have carried houses away, the structure required substantial safeguards. Foundations, frame and floors are all reinforced and, facing the sea wind, there is a deep pent eave that acts as an air foil.

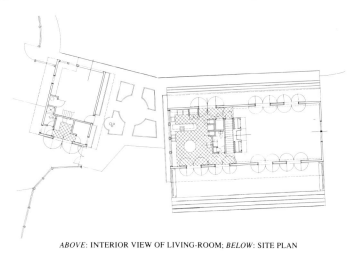

ABOVE: INTERIOR VIEW OF LIVING-ROOM; *BELOW*: SITE PLAN

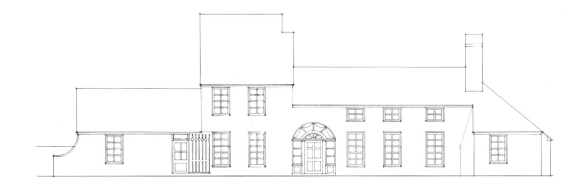

WINTERTHUR HOUSING, PROJECT, 1983
WILMINGTON, DELAWARE

We were asked to design four houses and a site plan for a rural parcel of land in a historic area of Northern Delaware. The houses were located on a new lane set back as far as possible from adjacent routes, leaving a great deal of the site as open field. The two-storey houses, designed to recall the complex massing and materials of traditional farm houses of the region, included garages, motorcourts and terraces that allowed for views of the surrounding farm land of the Winterthur Trust.

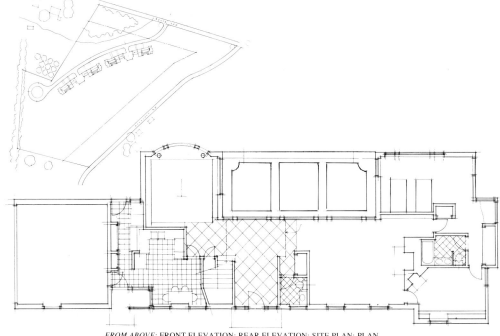

FROM ABOVE: FRONT ELEVATION; REAR ELEVATION; SITE PLAN; PLAN

HOUSE ON LONG ISLAND IV, 1983
GLEN COVE, NEW YORK

This house for a large, active family is on the North Shore, on a peninsula jutting into Long Island Sound with dramatic views of the Sound to the east and the New York City skyline to the west. The siting and plan are designed to take advantage of these views.

The house is anchored by two dense cores containing the stairs, fireplaces, cabinets and storage. The major living spaces are on the first floor. A grand living room at the peninsula end of the house offers a 270-degree panoramic view of Long Island Sound. This room has a domed ceiling, eyebrow dormers and a massive fireplace. The broad roof overhang forms a sheltered porch that wraps around the living level.

The ground floor contains the entry, a three-car garage, maid's room, a game room, and a lap pool with

exercise and bathroom area. The upstairs bedroom level is crammed with complex spaces like those of a yacht. Children's and guest rooms are located over the family room. The master bedroom suite is open to views of the east and west and has a balcony overlooking the living room.

The house has a bold and simple form that sits proudly on the lawn. Its concrete base recalls the massive stone rip-rap protecting the peninsula. The base is punctuated on the east by small windows for morning light in the lap pool, and on the west and north by a protected entry arcade. The lower roof and exterior walls are clad with silver-grey cedar shingles. The upper roof is covered by lead-coated copper that unites the circular and rectilinear parts of the house.

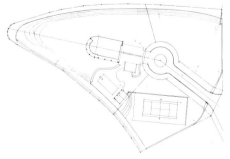

ABOVE: VIEW OF HOUSE FROM DRIVEWAY; *BELOW*: SITE PLAN

ABOVE AND BELOW: VIEWS OF HOUSE FROM GARDEN

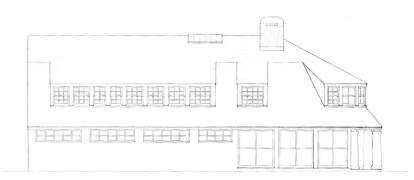

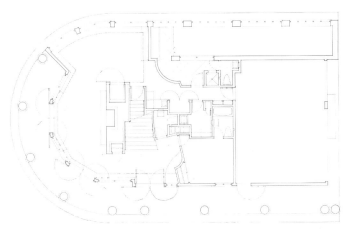
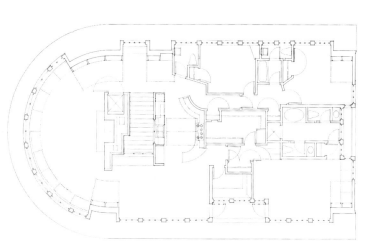

ABOVE: SIDE ELEVATIONS; *MIDDLE*: VIEW THROUGH COLONNADE AND LIVING-ROOM; *BELOW*: GROUND AND FIRST-FLOOR PLANS

CHANGING FAMILY FORMS

DENISE SCOTT BROWN

My father was one of seven siblings, my mother one of five, and I am one of four. I grew up in a suburban house that accommodated our family and for varying lengths of time, aunts, uncles, grandparents, cousins and a lodger. For a few years we had an aunt, a grandmother and a lodger living with us at the same time. Two grandmothers died in our house. My grandfather and two families of cousins lived reasonably close to us and visiting was frequent. Family festivities and religious observances took place in my grandfather's house and later in ours.

This accessible, extended family had enormous impact on my childhood. It relieved the tightness of the nuclear family and provided alternative forms of support and nurturing, other repertoires of family arrangements, additional role models, and, in general, more information on everything from careers to clothes. Staying with cousins was a liberating experience. They were part of us but in some ways different. They enlarged my vocabulary of what was possible and helped me to define and redefine myself by matching against close and loved but different people. Older cousins led us to adventure. (Younger cousins, like younger siblings, were merely boring.) Aunts and uncles were exciting, mythic characters. Their careers and interests loomed larger than life and were more visible, because less protected, than those of our parents.

My grandmother's room in our house was a totally different place. There was time in there. A low west sun shone in while she listened to the evening news on the radio. We could join her over milk and cookies in the late afternoon after school and talk to her while she made things. I learned a great deal about the world as my grandmother sewed, listened to the radio, and exclaimed about the news. A room in our house was occupied by our lodger and was known by his name. It had an air of urbane sophistication that suggested night life and 'girl friends'. When he left, it was occupied by pairs of British sailors on leave from wartime duty. They had been around the world. One had an opal taken from an Indian temple. The room was renamed 'the sailors' room'.

Our house was at the edge of the suburbs. There was an empty field beside us that was still 'countryside'. I could ride my bicycle to school and the local stores but it was a long car or bus ride to town, where my father worked. Though we were proud of his work, we didn't know what he did. Sometimes on Saturdays he took us to his office, but it was always empty when we were there.

As a student and young architect living and working in Europe, I shared the homes of friends and colleagues in many different countries in what (I now realise) was a search for my own preferred family type. Although most were nuclear families, there were differences in custom, ritual, and patterns of deference. Particularly interesting was the family of the architect for whom I worked in Rome. The family living quarters and work place were combined in one large apartment. While we young architects of his *gruppo* worked at our drawing boards in the studio, Carolina, the baby, propelled herself between us in her wheeled chair. We babysat while drawing. Now and then, while we were all engaged in discussion, the baby (who is now an architect) would get into the drawing basket. We kept a careful eye on thumb tacks. The architect's wife was also his secretary and business manager.

Sadly, there was a retarded son. Somehow the son was managed as well in the apartment-workplace. We learned to be understanding and learned how to treat him.

The bathroom of our employer's apartment was a boon to us, because there was no hot water in the room we rented in a seven-storey walk-up in another part of Rome. Like many Romans, we would go once a week to a 'day hotel' for a good hot shower. The hot water bath was still a public rather than a private facility in Rome. The best baths, in the new station building, were known grandiosely as the Roman Baths.

Cold water was available to us in the apartment that we shared with the Roman family and we could heat water in their kitchen for morning coffee. Our landlords appeared to be an extended family. Every evening they would play cards in the living room. Their nine-year old son played with the rest of the family and went to bed as late as any of them, around one AM. The next morning he would set off to school, earlier than any of them, in his black cotton smock and white collar. He was like a small adult and took the family responsibility of politeness to us equally upon his shoulders. Italian children seemed more adult and less pressured than English or American children. I sensed that this related in some way to the Italian family's view of work. It was as if the whole family had a job of work to do, besides its job of child rearing, and that sharing in this responsibility allowed the children to feel a measure of self respect within the family that is not available in cultures where work is separate from the home.

This is true, perhaps internationally, for farm families and the kids in mom and pop stores. Some academic and professional families achieve similar relationships between work life and family life, and I remember a rural family in central Yugoslavia who served us a meal while all members sat in a circle around us threading tobacco leaves. I visited a family in Spain where the sewing machine had pride of place in the living room and the mother stitched shoe uppers as her son entertained us.

Travel pointed up different types of relation between home and the outside world. The institutionalisation of bathing as a non-domestic activity is common to many cultures; schooling of the young outside the home, to most. In villages in Yugoslavia there were public ovens for villagers' casseroles but sewage disposal was often a private, quite informal activity.

Living in the United States, I continued my participant observation of family forms and my unconscious building of preferences for my own family life, adding my professional interest because family patterns relate to architecture and urban planning. Although few American families were as exotic as some of the European ones, there were fascinating comparisons to be made between ethnic American forms and their counterparts in their countries of origin. American ethnic patterns seemed to be European 19th-century patterns that had often been replaced in the mother country. It was interesting, too, to meet my American second cousins and to see how similar their family customs were to those of my family overseas.

My husband and I married late. By that time we were both well-set in our careers, my family had resettled on another continent, and his – except for his mother who lived near us – were too far away for frequent meetings. When we adopted a baby, we lacked the family support systems I had known as a child. Nevertheless, we have fashioned substitutes and have evolved our own working relations with the institutions that support and augment American family life.

Bob and I have a joint career in child-raising, home-making, architecture and urban planning. In our professional lives, we are two of three partners in a 50-person firm. At home, we have devised an extended family unit and a support system that goes beyond it. There is no clear seam between our work and family lives, both because we prefer it that way and because it makes our lives possible.

To maintain close ties between work and home, we originally tried to find a large old house that could be converted to an architects' office and allow room for an apartment for us above it. However, houses that suited our taste and the size of our office were invariably in areas zoned residential, where waivers would not have been granted for a professional firm. Eventually we found our dream house. It had stood vacant for two years, and was looked upon by its owner as a large, old, white elephant that had to be sold before he could subdivide the valuable property at its front for suburban, split-level, colonial, ranch houses.

Our house is in an old suburb within the city boundary. It is in an integrated neighbourhood of primarily professional people who zealously protect both the neighbourhood's integration and its residential character. The neighbourhood is outstandingly well served by schools. The white elephant to its previous owner is a historic Art Nouveau house to us, set in an English Romantic landscape. To our friends it is known as 'the Garden of the Finzi-Venturi'. Working to restore and maintain, furnish, and decorate this house is part of our family job, one closely tied to our professional lives. As our work precludes the possibility of weekends at the shore or long vacations, we can't be a two-house family. Our year-round home must double as our vacation place.

We have a housekeeper who lives in during the week. She has been with us more than ten years, is a grandmother, and is virtually a third parent in our household. We rent a small apartment in our basement to an architecture student who partly pays his rent by helping around the house and yard. Every spring, we advertise in schools of architecture for a handy-person, to live with us during the summer and help restore the house and maintain the yard. In addition, two elderly ladies help out on occasion, and the cook in our local restaurant uses his spare time in the afternoon to fetch our child from school and do the ferrying that suburban mothers do.

This is our basic ersatz family. We have had eight handy-people. They are about the ages of the children Bob and I would have now, if we had had a normal family cycle. Most have become our very good friends. Several have joined our firm and the first now runs our New York office. As our son grows older, the handy-people assume a tutorial role in addition to their household functions, replacing the distant aunts and uncles that I found so important in my life. Jimmie can be packed off to spend a few days with one or two of them much as I went to visit my aunt. He has found, as well, a grandmother substitute in one of our elderly helpers and has made a private arrangement with her to bake his birthday cakes.

On occasion, our house is as full as any Victorian augmented-family house with visiting cousins, grandparents, and helpful handy-people. More often the guest room is occupied by visiting colleagues from all over the world. Once a year we fly to Europe to vacation with my parents. We are usually joined by several of Jimmie's cousins, the sons and daughters of my siblings. My parents' apartment, in an urban high-rise complex, epitomises the *Ville Radieuse* image of urbanism. I ponder the fact that this model has proved so successful for the international neighbours of my parents (including families with small children and expatriate American families) and so disastrous in America.

Our office is two miles from our house. When we moved from centre city we were apprehensive about cutting our ties with downtown services and contacts. However, we have managed to establish the work patterns and linkages needed to operate professionally in the outskirts. In any case, we are within a few blocks of the expressway that goes downtown and to the airport. Our clients seem to have no trouble finding us, our hearts and dispositions are happier for not having to battle through traffic twice a day, and we can go home at lunch time for a rest. Various children, including ours, find their way into our office, particularly over weekends. Though we try to protect our employees from their onslaught, we are happy the children have found more ersatz uncles and aunts and some excellent role models. When Jimmie runs on Main Street, I can keep an eye on him from my office window and the owner of the corner store will do the same for me from her window. If I am out of town on business and something goes wrong with my daily arrangements for Jimmie, the secretaries in our office, who have their own children, will set in motion my back-up systems.

I do no supermarket shopping. A small local provisioner takes my order by telephone every Friday morning and delivers into our refrigerator on Saturdays. Jimmie attended a co-op nursery school and now a co-op Sunday school. I am on the adult education and curriculum committees and go to school with him on Sunday mornings. The neighbourhood has a food co-op but I don't have time to belong. Our immediate neighbours and fellow co-opers are another important part of our family's support system. They are our clan group.

My mother-in-law was afraid that we would put her 'away in a home for old ladies' – and we eventually did. By that time she was quite senile; but I came to feel she would have been much happier had she spent a few more of her last years there than she did. That bustling, friendly place would have solved her need for companionship and abated her fear of being alone much better than we could. When we visited, we would bring Jimmie, then two years old, and wheel Bob's mother and her room-mate into the public space beside the elevators. Here Jimmie would receive a dozen or more instant grandparents; even senile people would make sense when approached by a small child. I came to see senility in a different light and our small son loved to operate wheelchairs. I found myself, once, in the strange situation of comforting an old lady whose children were planning to take her away from the home to live with them. 'I'm sure you'll find other friends, Mary,' I said. By the time my mother-in-law died, Jimmie had another grand-mother substitute, 91 years older than himself, and we had found a good friend. We continued to visit her until she died.

Our family isn't typical but it has organised itself to meet the changing forces that are altering all American families. It has been shaped, as well, by our house and neighbourhood. These shaping forces and physical forms are central to the concerns of architects and planners.

Immigration, migration, industrialisation, and economic, occupational and social mobility have acted as detribalising and secularising forces on American families. Recently, the economic recession, the increased entry of women into the work force, the two-paycheque family, and the ideals of the women's movement have put further pressure for change on the family. Society has reacted by shifting the balance, once again, between what is considered private and what public. Care of young children is in the process of being institutionalised, not without trauma. Co-operative groups formed for schooling, child care, consumption, and living seem to be efforts to evolve support systems that can substitute for the missing family and tribe. The communes of the 1960s were early and colourful attempts at family substitutes. Less spectacularly, Americans have tended toward social and affective groups that lie somewhere between family and tribe. These have coalesced around neighbourhood concerns (cooperative nursery schools), religious practice (the Havura movement), age cohorts (homes for the elderly), and shared problems (single parent clubs).

Housing markets, and to some extent housing patterns, are changing as a result of changing family forms and shifting economic conditions. Suburban rental homes, condominiums in the city, single person home ownership, and all-adult communities are manifestations of these changes. Family emotional support and 'eldering' have long been institutionalised through psychiatry, which has blossomed into family therapy, marriage counselling, child psychiatry, and related services in family social work, foster care, and protection for battered family members. Other traditional, though less desirable, supports for the maintenance of some families persist: prostitution and the extra-marital relationship.

The communal kitchens and rearranged housing plans that were foreseen and desired by early suffragists have not materialised outside the kibbutz. Movement has been in another direction, towards the domestication of the work place. Part-time and shared time work, parental leaves, pressure against economic mobility exerted by the other spouse's job, and whole-family co-operative child care, are family-derived influences and work arrangements that threaten to change the work place, socially and physically. A similar reasserting of family values is occurring in other aspects of life, through co-ops in education and consumption.

This process of redomestication should be understood and aided by planners. Family substitutes and support networks are necessary in a mass society precisely because the help of families, clans and tribes cannot always be present or effective. The institutions that have evolved to augment family support are necessary and will not go away. However, there should be ways of making them part of the family. If grandma is in a home for the elderly, then the whole family should be there too. A warm aura of welcome should pervade grandma's room and she should have the dignity of playing hostess, even if she is senile. Homes for the elderly should provide small juice bars just off the public way, where grandparents can serve fruit juice to their grandchildren. If Mums and Dads go to work then kids should on occasion go there too. Day care facilities should be available close to parents' work places.

As family patterns and institutional relations change, so planners can expect change in use of the existing housing stock. For example, Victorian housing that is too large for the nuclear family could be well used, once again, when families double up to cope with economic recession or rising energy bills. Zoning should control but not proscribe this. Imaginative combinations of zoning categories, for example, 'professional-residential,' could assure the continued life of some fine residences. The 'professional' category could go beyond the now permitted doctor's office, on condition that at least one principal in the professional firm live 'above the store'.

New housing, in the near future, is likely to be constrained more by economic conditions than by family forms, and a new house will be an option for fewer families of any type. Both economics and demography will dictate smaller units, multiple units, and locations that are convenient to work and facilities.

When considering questions of housing type and zoning, professional planners must judge whether their own value orientation is the only one suitable in a given case. Planners who consider themselves too sophisticated to 'ram their aesthetic tastes down the throats of other cultures' may still be indignant at the thought of 'putting old people away' in homes. However, old people, like all other people, have varied tastes. Some want to live in adult communities, others enjoy well-run old age homes, some want to

be with their families, and others want to be alone. In the rooming house I occupied as a graduate student, we had a fellow roomer who was 84. She refused to live in the suburbs with her daughter because she liked to walk to the corner store. The dental student on her floor kept an eye on her. Planners should offer maximum feasible choice by evolving complex housing strategies containing many opportunities. Our home-made family arrangements would be anathema to many of our friends and, indeed, nostalgia for the Victorian family should not obscure the fact that some of its members found it constricting and debilitating. Planners should be particularly aware of the web of ties that supports marginal families and substitutes for or augments welfare programmes in stable, low-income neighbourhoods.

Changing family forms and the diversity of today's family types should be recognised in all areas of planning. For example, health planners should understand that some families will bring the baby to the hospital accompanied by five other children and grandma, or not come at all. This can be an opportunity to check the health of the whole family. Commercial planners should realise that working mothers need to take the kids to buy shoes between seven and nine PM on week-nights. We haven't even begun to consider yet the effect on family life of the 500-dollar home computer tied into your television screen.

Architects should redefine the ideal home. There is room again in architecture for utopian thinking. It should focus on serving changing living conditions and family forms. A new openness in the minds and eyes of architects should help their ideals to be pragmatic ones and their utopias to be humane.

Family-based design prototypes for the 1980s are more likely to appear in schools of architecture than in developers' offices or housing agencies. These designs should update the tradition of housing utopias of the 19th and early 20th centuries. If their point of departure is the family, they should hark back particularly to the housing designs of the early feminists.[1] However, a new contribution from architects today would be to spell out the physical implications of humanist and feminist aims to domesticate the world outside the home. Architects' designs should show that we can make the larger world good for families by producing home-like institutions and work places as well as workable homes.

Few architects will have the privilege of designing new housing for changing family types. A more real prospect is replanning and rehabilitating existing residential neighbourhoods to permit linkages between work, home, institutions, and services that will facilitate today's family living.

Architects should continue to rethink the family home. Some architects see commissions for private houses as opportunities to evolve paradigms for housing. By confronting problems that are general to many families, they hope their designs will have moral force beyond the needs of their individual clients. The applicability of such designs may be limited but they are often the only way of erecting signposts to the future. They should not be scorned.

With accelerating change in family patterns, a case can be made for housing forms that are adaptable, to suit families that must themselves adapt to economic and technological change. For such families, the symbol of home may be more permanent than its form or function; therefore prototype designs for their homes should not ignore the symbolic dimension. Learning what home means to families may help ease the transition when families change.

This article appeared in the Journal of the American Planning Association *Spring 1983, pp133-37. I thank Professor Geoffrey H Steere, of the American Studies Programme, University of Kansas, for sharing his views on the history and condition of the American family.*

Notes

1 See Dolores Hayden, *The Grand Domestic Revolution: A History of Feminist Designs for American Homes, Neighbourhoods and Cities,* MIT, Cambridge, Mass, 1981.

HOUSING PROTOTYPES FOR AUSTIN, TEXAS
DENISE SCOTT BROWN

The Republic Square District is the new name for Austin's warehouse district, built in the 1930s and 40s. Its site, on Town Lake, was also the birth place of Austin, where its founders aimed to build 'a truly National City'. We were asked by a development company, intending donors of property for the Laguna Gloria Art Museum, to help select a site for the Museum and produce a plan for the District. We worked on the District plan from 1983-85, while we were in the early stages of design of the Museum.

The Company's vision was of a mixed-use district accommodating, not only the next phase of growth of the downtown, but also community, cultural and recreational facilities, retail uses and housing. Some key assumptions of the plan were (to quote from our report):

The major location for growth of the Austin downtown over the next ten years will be the Republic Square District. Within the District lies 60 per cent of the CBD's capacity to carry new retail and office uses.

Although developing this area of Austin may be less simple and more expensive than developing outlying areas, it is a challenging and exciting prospect. Development in the District is important to the city because it would greatly increase the urban tax base and because the urban infrastructure and capacity are available there now. Rational growth management suggests increasing intensity where infrastructure and capacity exist before investing in new infrastructure in the suburbs.

To ensure the success of the development, a hierarchical organisation of existing streets and an extension of Third Street across Shoal Creek are needed to tie the District into the downtown region. Plans for parking and extension of transit will reinforce plans for street improvement and traffic management.

Within the District, a mix of public and private uses will set up linkages between activities at local and regional scale, and will bring about a network of pedestrian movement that reinforces the vitality of streets, public places and private buildings.

Important anchors to the district will be Republic Square with the Laguna Gloria Art Museum facing it on Fourth Street; the development along Third Street and the 'Rambla', linking Congress Avenue to Shoal Creek; and City Hall with its attendant open spaces.

Within the dictates of market, physical capacity and regulations, the District will be developed to its full potential, though not necessarily to the 'highest and best' use for any individual block. Decisions on density and use will be made to achieve maximum benefit, district-wide and over time. The balance of lower densities on some blocks with higher densities on others is a valuable form of subsidy for which city support will be sought.

Certain 'non-economic' uses, the Laguna Gloria Art Museum, child care and medical emergency centres, aged health care facilities, convenience shopping and housing, can help achieve amenity, stability, and a higher urban economy in the long run. Financial mechanisms will be investigated to make such uses feasible.

Housing is needed in the District as a basic constituent of the type of environment we aim to generate and as a support for its other functions. There are many reasons to advocate housing in the inner city. Not the least is to support office uses beyond the capacities of available parking; also to share parking, patronise the Museum, broaden the market for retail uses and the enliven the Rambla.

Housing prototypes were developed for eight blocks at the western edge of the District, near or alongside Shoal Creek (see key map). The report describes them by block and type:

Blocks 23, 24, 25, 26, 47, 48, 49 and 50 are identified with the creek and with residential uses and services. Blocks 23 and 24 are shown joined together to form one long narrow block that ends at the creek. For the sake of the overall, the Rambla should continue across the front of block 23-24. The dimensions of this combination would be 93ft x 484ft. Ground-floor use should be service, including health and medical service, convenience retail for the residential area, and possibly the peripatetic four-screen movie theatre. The end of the block beside Shoal Creek should include a creek-and-trail restaurant with a ground floor platform and second floor balcony overlooking the creek. Another predominantly second floor use could be a small branch library for the District or a health club. A two-level below-grade parking garage could hold 360 cars.

Block 26 has been considered for office or residential use. We have submitted several residential plans for this block. Most involve an east-west facing slab with town housing in the remaining area. Two levels of below-ground parking are shown. The top level may protrude above ground on the north and west sides of the block to enable the townhouses to be raised a few feet and therefore to gain privacy for their street-facing windows. On the Rambla side and on San Antonio Street, retail uses that need ground-floor access can be adjusted within the slope on the property. Ground-floor uses on Third Street should be convenience retail for residential and office users. On San Antonio there could be a health club. If block 26 becomes an office building, it should be considered part of The Rambla District and Rambla guidelines would apply. The office tower should orient north south. Both housing and office use of block 26 can be supported in planning and urban design terms, and the market will probably dictate which it becomes. The point at which it is built in the staging sequence could have planning implications.

We recommend closing sections of Fourth and Rio Grande Streets before they hit the Creek to join blocks 25, 47 and 48. We have shown three alternative forms of housing for such a project. Those that would probably be most marketable now in Austin may not be economically feasible given the cost of land. The portion of the site that adjoins the Creek could be planned for passive recreation and could accommodate two small child-care centres, one off Third Street, and the other off Rio Grande Street.

Other forms of housing we investigated are the 'townhouse maze' and the 'mini-megastructure'. The first cannot achieve the density required by the economic programme. The second can but may not be marketable. Blocks where we feel the high density of housing required for economic reasons could be achieved are: 48 and 25, because they are Creek related; 26, because it is part of the high density Rambla; and 2, because it looks out over Town Lake and would be close to City Hall and the Rambla.

Escalating land costs will drive housing out of the District unless financial mechanisms can be found to fill the gap between land values and affordable housing. Transfer of development rights or of floor area ratio allowances between blocks could be one direction for investigation. Co-operation with non-profit groups that build housing for the elderly is another. If housing cannot be made economically feasible as a predominant use on several District blocks, perhaps it can be included as a penthouse use on some blocks. This, however, would not provide a critical mass of demand that would extend the market for other uses in the District.

The extracts cited here are taken from A Plan for the Republic Square District Austin, Texas, *prepared for the Watson-Casey Companies by Venturi, Rauch and Scott Brown in May 1984.*

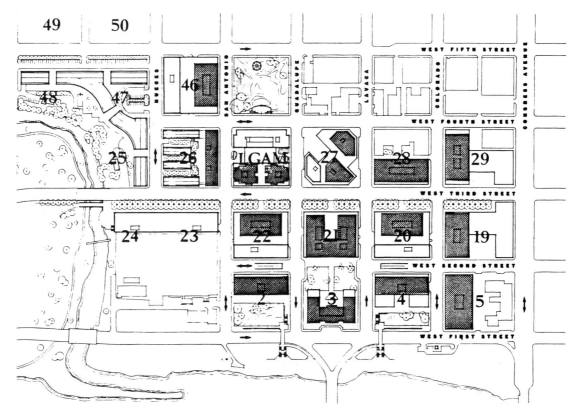

SITE PLAN, REPUBLIC SQUARE DISTRICT

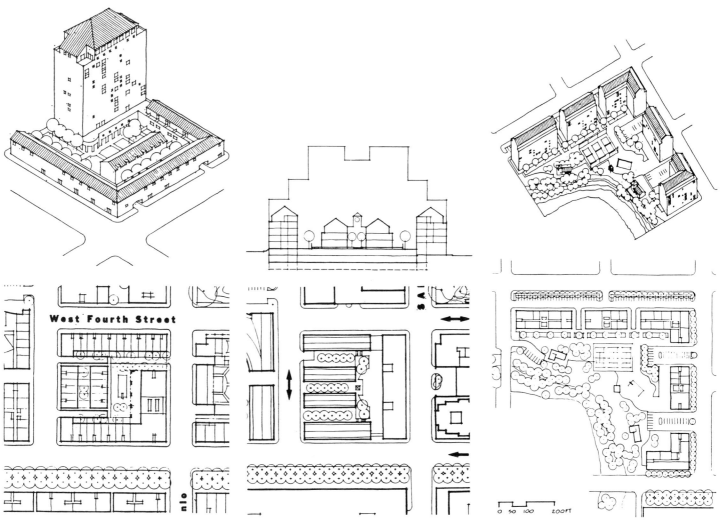

ABOVE AND BELOW, LEFT TO RIGHT: BLOCK 26, 'SOCIETYHILL' HOUSING; BLOCK 26, 'HILLOCK' HOUSING; BLOCKS 25, 47 AND 48, 'BOULEVARD' HOUSING

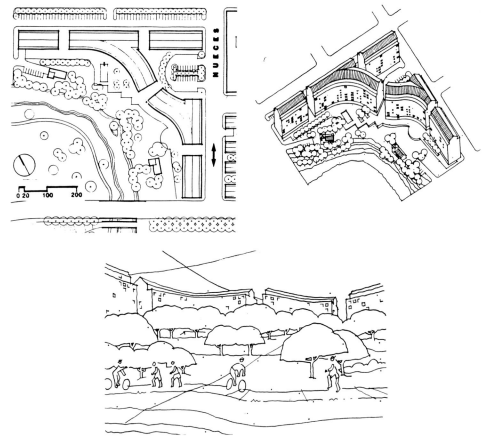

ABOVE: BLOCKS 25, 47 AND 48, 'MIDRISE' HOUSING; *BELOW*: VIEW OF MIDRISE HOUSING

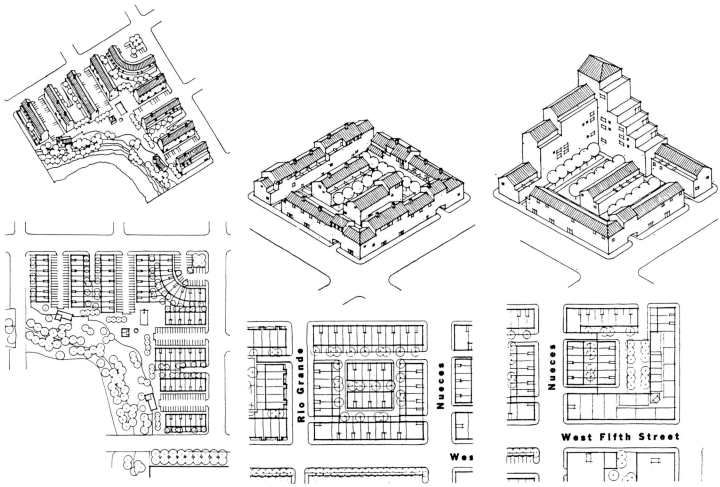

ABOVE AND BELOW, LEFT TO RIGHT: BLOCKS 25, 47 AND 48, 'TOWNHOUSES'; BLOCK 50, 'TOWNHOUSE MAZE'; BLOCK 51, 'MINI-MEGA' HOUSING

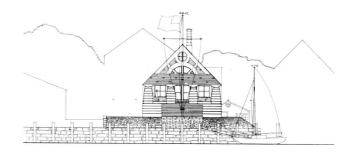

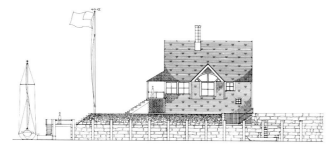

ABOVE: WATERFRONT ELEVATION; *MIDDLE*: VIEW OF MAIN FACADE; *BELOW*: EAST ELEVATION

HOUSE AT STONY CREEK, 1984
STONY CREEK, CONNECTICUT

Designed by Steven Izenour

The client, a couple in their sixties, had spent summers on one of the nearby Thimble Islands for thirty years. The programme and zoning dictated a one-storey house, elevated to protect against hurricanes and floods. The area's strong winter winds mandated an internal garage. The owners required a living room designed around their collections of Piranesi and theatrical drawings and a sophisticated sound system for their collection of operas.

An almost square, simple bungalow plan with gable roof was chosen for its compact efficiency and scale and profile sympathetic with its neighbours. The large 'rose-window' ship wheel on the north facade presents a public-scale entrance. The entry vestibule works around the central fireplace to open into the 35-foot-high living room with vaulted ceiling. Four flat Doric columns on the full-width porch frame Long Island Sound and the rock-bound islands beyond. From the water, the house recalls a Classical Revival bungalow. On the east and west elevations a diagonal, all-over pattern of white, scalloped shingles creates a Victorian decorative scale. The cedar shingle exterior has weathered over the years to a silver grey.

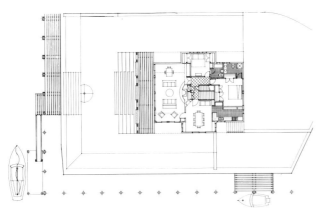
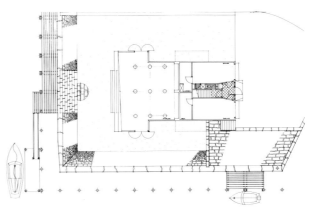

ABOVE: EXTERIOR VIEW OF HOUSE FROM REAR AND VIEW OF LIVING-ROOM; *BELOW*: FIRST AND GROUND-FLOOR PLANS

ABOVE AND BELOW: INTERIOR VIEWS OF UPPER AND LOWER STOREYS

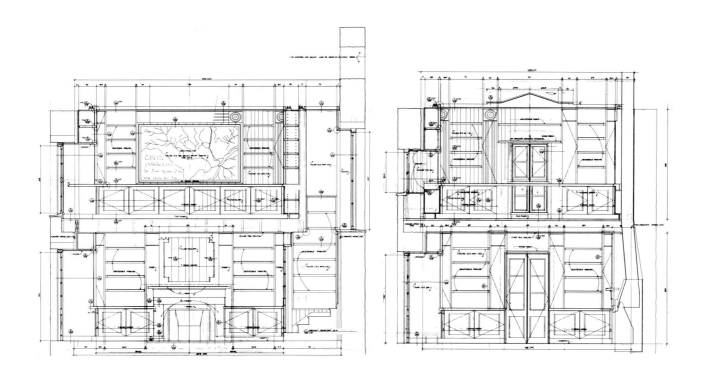

LIBRARY FOR A HOUSE IN NORTHERN ITALY, 1984
LAKE ORTA, ITALY

This project forms a new lining within a 200-year-old stone-walled and roofed barn characteristic of its locale and of great quality.

The client requested a two-storey domestic library with Empire-style references. The references are abstracted, stylised, representational, and generous in scale.

The play of layers in this small building is also a counter-point of inside with outside, structure with cladding, and rustic grandeur with urbane precision.

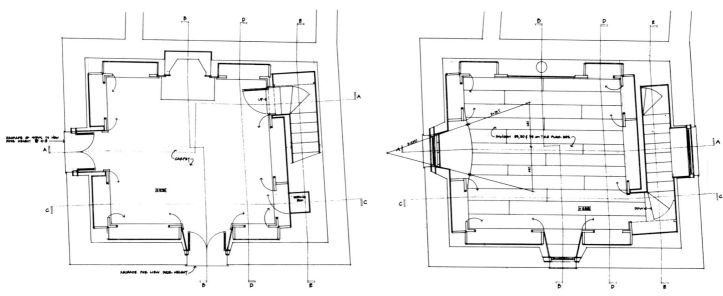

ABOVE: SECTION ELEVATIONS; *BELOW*: GROUND AND FIRST-FLOOR PLANS

SUNSHINE DREAM VILLAGE, PROJECT, 1985
ORLANDO, FLORIDA

The Sunshine Foundation, a Philadelphia-based non-profit organisation, helps bring joy to terminally ill children and their families by granting each a special wish. Because most children choose to visit Disney World, Florida, the Foundation commissioned the design of a vacation complex there for seven families. The new facility was to have a special fairy tale, dreamlike quality.

Our design combines functional aspects of the old Florida motor court with the fantasy of the Snow White story. The Family House is for gathering and dining. The Seven Dwarf Houses are individual bungalows planned to accommodate the needs of sick children and wheelchairs. At the centre of the village are a playground, barbecue and landscaped foot paths. A service road at the perimeter gives ambulance access to all bungalows.

ABOVE: VIEW OF COURTYARD; *BELOW*: ELEVATIONS

PEARL HOUSES, 1985
WEST PALM BEACH, FLORIDA

This prototype design is the basis for a series of houses offered by Warren Pearl Development Corporation near West Palm Beach, Florida. The design provides buyers with numbers of options that allow them to 'customise' *their version of the house. These options include a choice between one or two storeys, variable window placements, different fireplace and entrance designs, and various detailing elements.*

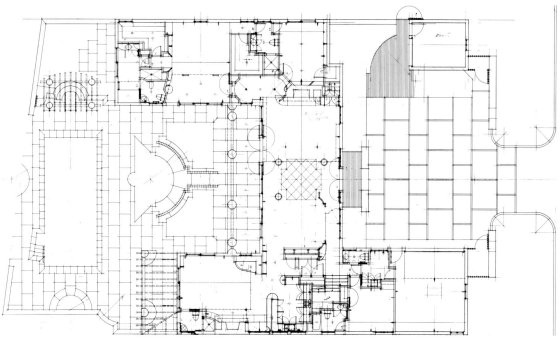

ABOVE: FRONT VIEW; *BELOW*: GROUND-FLOOR PLAN

OPPOSITE: VIEW OF OPEN PLAN LIVING-SPACE; *ABOVE*: SIX DIFFERENT HOUSES PRESENTING ALTERNATIVE VARIATIONS IN FIREPLACES, ELEVATIONS AND ENTRANCES

MEMPHIS: A HOUSING STRATEGY
DENISE SCOTT BROWN

These are excerpts from an essay for the 'Memphis 1948-1958' exhibition, at the Memphis Brooks Museum, in 1986, and from the housing section of a Downtown Development Plan for Memphis, initiated in 1984 by the Memphis Center City Commission (CCC). Taken together, they illustrate an approach to housing and the city that is culturally based and finely tuned to local conditions.

FROM MEMPHIS DOWN THE MISSISSIPPI TO THE WORLD
Memphis and 'Maimfeez'

When a gathering of avant-garde Milanese designers paused a minute to think up a name for their new group, it was no coincidence that the music in the background suggested the name Memphis, or, said with an Italian accent, Maimfeez. Barbara Radice has recounted in her book on the group: 'There was a Bob Dylan record on, "Stuck Inside of Mobile with the Memphis Blues Again" and since nobody bothered to change the record, Bob Dylan went on howling "the Memphis Blues Again" until Sottsass said, "Okay, let's call it Memphis", and everybody thought it was a great name: Blues, Tennessee, rock 'n' roll, American suburbs, and then Egypt, the Pharaohs' capital, the holy city of the god Ptah.'[1]

Memphis on the record player in that Milanese apartment in December 1980 represented cool sophistication, about as cool as you could get, and perhaps high-culture aristocratic disdain, which elevates elements of popular culture to artistic acclaim and disassociates itself from the earnest, middle culture that lies between.

In design circles today, the word 'Memphis' brings to mind multi-coloured, lyrical objects that have their origin in furniture and tableware but are more or less unusable. The cultural roots of Memphis design are as eclectic as those of Memphis music. Memphis style springs from the German Bauhaus, but comes via America, and the Americanised

Bauhaus strain we call Depression Modern. The Milanese designers embraced the popular form of this strain: Googie. Googie dates from the 1950s. It was the style of Formica and tubular steel kitchen and patio furniture, kidney-shaped backyard pools and table-mats, and particularly of the famous Holiday Inn sign and the decor of early Holiday Inns, which had their genesis in Memphis. Patterned Formica, curving tubes and kidney shapes set the tone for Maimfeez, as they did for Googie culture.

In Milan, the music of Memphis stood for all this. In London, too, in the mid 50s, there were ducktail haircuts and 'skiffle' groups of young musicians playing spontaneously (or almost spontaneously) on street corners and in underground trains. Soon rock and roll was everywhere and, out of Liverpool, a working class culture, perhaps even more eclectic than Elvis, emerged. Elvis, then the Beatles, danced down the electronic waves and over the world. Low art met high art as the chic and the avant-garde embraced what had been the music of the poor, the oppressed, the regional and the local.

Geography as Destiny
If Memphis culture welled up from the soil of the Mississippi, gelled on Beale Street and danced world-wide with Elvis, other Memphis artefacts had travelled that route before.

Riding into the city, you pass vast rail marshalling yards and piggy-back truck and coach storage lots. Federal Express is a strong presence at the airport; complexes of barges go by on the Mississippi. Memphis has long been a major distribution centre.

Break-of-bulk points, where goods are transshipped from wagon to steamer or rail to truck, have historically been points of origin of cities. Memphis, at a rare site on the Mississippi where the bluffs rise above flood level, owes its economy and configuration to its topography. The distributive economy, which received and shipped crops, products and services long before it sent a regional culture to the world, has combined in spectacular ways with the geography. The beautiful view of Memphis from the Mississippi is one result, but there are others, more subtle: from office buildings in downtown Memphis, one looks out over the Chickasaw Bluff, onto the brown river and then beyond, at farm land. Where Philadelphians see Camden and New Yorkers see Hoboken, Memphians see the Mississippi flood plain, the prettiest green view that could be imagined from a downtown.

The closeness of the bluffs impeded riveredge development at the centre of Memphis. Where other cities hardened their river banks to provide flat land for rail beds and warehouses, Memphis' Cobblestones, the historic strand where the cotton embarked, is the hardest the downtown river line becomes. Along much of the urban shoreline, the river ripples against a soft bank. From the Cobblestones, mules dragged bales on Court and Monroe Streets to and from the city. These streets are wider than others in the Memphis

A PROPOSAL FOR THE

CENTER CITY
DEVELOPMENT PLAN
··· DOWNTOWN ···
MEMPHIS
TENNESSEE

VENTURI, RAUCH AND SCOTT BROWN
DACP ASSOCIATES
ARTHUR D. LITTLE, INC.
URBAN PARTNERS
WILLIAMSON/AWSUMB

MARCH 16, 1984

grid because the laden wagons had to zigzag up and down the steep slope.

Perhaps people who grow up on rivers learn to be canny. Remember Huck Finn. The river is an incessant problem and opportunity. It presents the challenge to think strategically, an urgent challenge because life and livelihood depend on the ability to use this resource to advantage. Without undue environmental determinism, one may speculate that river economies breed especially enterprising entrepreneurs. Consider the Memphis cotton factors. When the cotton market declined in the Mid-South, some Memphis merchants adapted their warehouses to the new crops in the region. Others concentrated on industries related to cotton and built up Memphis as a service and know-how centre for the cotton industry. Yet others marketed their real estate and became developers, and some followed the shifting cotton market where it led them, to Texas and later the Far East, becoming multi-national corporations. They went down the Mississippi to join the world economy.

A Cultural Crossroads

Culture followed cotton. Music of the cotton fields appears to have taken the agricultural routes to market, making Memphis a musical mixing bowl of the Mid-South. As happens in trade centres and despite the barriers of segregation, there occurred in Memphis a clash of cultures whose impact produced mutants of energy and beauty. On Beale Street, where urban met rural, Gospel met secular, folk met jazz and white met black, blues poured out. Beale Street became the centre of a variegated, multi-rooted, black artistic expression of world significance.

A further mutation occurred around Beale Street in the early 1950s, when a young, white Elvis somehow fitted himself into the black music picture. Through Elvis, black blues and rhythm-and-blues joined white country and Gospel music and the result was rock and roll. But canny entrepreneurs were there to see the importance of the mutation, support it and build on it. From the turn of the century, there had been a strong Jewish and Italian presence on Beale Street. If rock and roll was, symbolically, an alliance between Beale Street and Lauderdale Courts, then the Pinch District, home of Memphis' ethnic communities, had a hand in purveying the result to the world. The history of ethnic Memphis is still to be written.

History as Destiny

In the physical form of Memphis lie preserved the layers of its history. At its outset, the city grandly and eclectically took upon itself a name from the Nile. Ancient Egypt, then cotton, then the blues, then rock, have been consistent themes in the city's imagery. The decade 1948-1958 was one of the most formative for Memphis. As in other American cities, this was the time of the great change to the automobile and the consequent realignment between suburbs and city centre. The outline of today's city began to emerge in this

decade. Memphis' appearance on the world stage at the same time left only modest markings on the city itself – a few symbols were added in civic places, but Beale Street languished, Sun Records was hard to find and the great symbol, Graceland, was allowed to draw visitors out of the centre of Memphis. Elvis' pink Cadillac, in this context, is symbolic of Elvis *and* the American move to the suburbs.

Since 1958, another regional and supra-regional movement has profoundly turned tides in Memphis. The city is still grappling with the final picture it sends to the world of the happenings, fortunate as well as tragic, that occurred on its streets and balconies during the civil rights movement. Perhaps it speaks well for Memphis that its heart stood still after Martin Luther King's death. One effect has been to leave the outline of the 1950's city clearer than it is in other cities. As the centre starts a new life today, it grows on the base of the 1950's city.

The period of the 50s, which might be considered too near for nostalgia, is subject to enormous nostalgia. This may result from the sorrows of the 60s, or the early death of Elvis, or it may be because we feel, in Memphis and America, that the 1950s have something positive to give the 1980s. On the one hand, the 1950s represent our blindness to problems that were welling up and would spill over later, but, on the other, they represent, especially in Memphis, cross-cultural creativity and shared artistic talent. And they are near enough for many of us to have been there; we can still talk with the main actors in their drama.

Memphis Today

Although the Mississippi was the locus of downtown and the centre of Memphis in the 50s and 60s, by the 80s the river had become the city's western boundary. In downtown Memphis today, we have layers of history and leftovers of history, attempted ameliorations that failed and promising sections waiting to succeed. But there is a new will to regenerate the historic centre and a new consciousness of the river, symbolised by the lighting of the Hernando De Soto bridge.

The task of pulling all together is in part a cultural one, which involves continuing to make the creative links that join the black community to the white, the religious to the secular and Memphis to the world. A connection is being promulgated in Memphis today between the memories of Martin Luther King and of the war in Vietnam, which is in the healing spirit of those other cross-cultural ties. Similar imaginative links must be sought in stimulating the downtown economy and advancing the portion of the inner city community that lives in poverty, and Beale Street has, yet again, a role to play in this growth.

The debates now ongoing on the future of downtown Memphis demonstrate that the city desires a regeneration that is not only physical, economic and social, but also artistic and spiritual, and that contains within it the layers

of its crossroads history.

A HOUSING STRATEGY

To achieve the aim of a unique downtown that offers cultural and commercial facilities to the whole region, there is needed a local community to support these facilities and workplaces every day. If a high percentage of workers could reach jobs downtown by foot or by local bus, this would support plans for a transportation system that did not destroy the very fabric it was intended to reach. If housing formed part of every centre city sub-area, residential development could figure prominently in the strategy for linking activity centres and could help narrow the gaps that separate sections of centre city from each other and from surrounding neighbourhoods. For these reasons, a housing stock should be promoted in and near downtown. This stock should offer a range of types and facilities to suit a wide spectrum of incomes and lifestyles.

There is a need for downtown housing similar to that chosen by the families of executives and managers in areas such as Germantown. Apartment housing for singles, young marrieds and empty nesters is another important downtown type. Some of this housing can be in converted industrial and office structures, particularly for those who like unusual loft apartments and an artistic lifestyle. 'Affordable' housing for moderate-income workers is needed in a band that surrounds the core and serves both the city centre and the Medical Centre. Housing for low-income workers already exists in the public housing projects near the downtown; maintenance and rehabilitation of this housing should have the same priority as the provision of housing to attract the rich. Both are central elements of the city centre economic strategy.

Downtown and its environs offer a wealth of locations for various types of housing, from the core area and the Bluffs to South Beale and the Biomedical Research Zone (BRZ). Neighbourhoods that surround the city centre should be considered in the formulation of a housing strategy. These include the One Riverside Drive area, the South Bluffs, South Main, East Main, South Beale, Greenlaw, the Bayou area, North Mud Island, the Pinch, and many others, stretching as far as midtown. Each has its own distinctive character, based in part on its heritage of existing buildings and their relation to topography. Each can form a unique neighbourhood with its own particular mix of housing types and a cluster of convenience retail, cultural, and community facilities that serve it. The combination of different neighbourhoods will permit the city centre to offer a much greater choice of housing types and lifestyles than its suburban competitors can.

The housing strategy envisions continuation of residential conversions of commercial, office and warehouse structures in the core, South Main and South Bluffs districts, as well as new construction on sites that offer stunning river views. Recommendations for residential development on the bluffs, North Mud Island, and North Main and Front Streets north of the Convention Centre, depend on the attraction of the Mississippi and Wolf Rivers. To preserve historic areas and protect views, there is provision for new high-rise housing near the Mississippi, at the northern and southern edges of Center City.

However, there are limitations to a downtown strategy confined narrowly to the city's western edge; therefore the plan recommends creating new 'in town' communities in and around the Biomedical Research Zone, by bringing old neighbourhoods back into the orbit of downtown, and by re-establishing linkages with downtown's original 'street car' suburb, Midtown.

These provisions of the housing strategy are based on a residential market analysis[2] whose main recommendations were:

Pursue a housing strategy that encourages a variety of housing types and addresses the particular needs of different income groups in and around the city centre.

Continue to support expanded riverfront and riverview housing at its current modest rate over the next five to ten years while protecting the river's edge for public use and enhancing both pedestrian and office views and access to the water.

Strongly support adaptive re-use of commercial buildings as new office development comes on the market, by co-ordinating the improvement of in-town residential neighbourhoods and by supporting infill housing and services to link conversions together.

Aggressively promote major new in-town development of mid-moderate income housing, to link downtown with the Medical Centre and provide a critical mass of broadened housing opportunities.

Support the development of North Mud Island as a relatively low-density residential community, comparable to other suburban developments and linked to the downtown for retail, entertainment and work-place services.

Support public housing modernisation, and rehabilitation and neighbourhood revitalisation in the ring of inner city neighbourhoods surrounding the downtown.

RECOMMENDATIONS FOR SUB-AREAS
Centre city and its neighbourhoods provide a wealth of locations for various types of housing, each with its own distinctive character. Together they can offer choices of housing types and lifestyles to a wide spectrum of population groups. We have listed recommendations for 17 different sub-areas, some within centre city and the purview of the study but some beyond. The recommendations are made from the viewpoint of centre city and to reinforce the goals of the Center City Development Plan. There may need to be discussion between local communities and centre city to discover whether some recommendations are acceptable as part of community plans.

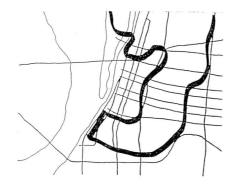

A HORSE-SHOE OF HOUSING AROUND DOWNTOWN

Downtown Core
In this area some old, high-rise office buildings are suitable candidates for conversion to housing and this is desirable in order to maintain occupancy in newer office buildings. Such conversions lend themselves to housing for singles, married couples without children, and empty nesters.

The market, the characteristics of the individual building, and the location will dictate whether the conversion should be for rental, co-op, or condominium apartments; the possibility of producing some rent-assisted units for low-moderate-income singles and couples, young or elderly, should be investigated.

The installation of public improvements should be timed to support conversions and rehabilitations to housing in the core, in order to augment the amenity of the growing in-town residential environment.

West Beale
On either side of Beale Street west of Main are opportunities for high-rise housing. Waterford Place already exists and Orpheum Plaza Towers is planned. In this restricted area, high-rise housing oriented towards the river is suitable and forms part of the east-west 'channel' for intense new growth recom-

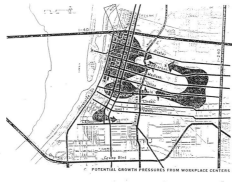

C POTENTIAL GROWTH PRESSURES FROM WORKPLACE CENTERS

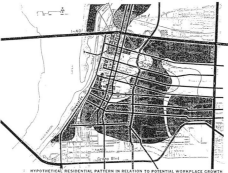

HYPOTHETICAL RESIDENTIAL PATTERN IN RELATION TO POTENTIAL WORKPLACE GROWTH

mended in the plan.

The housing type is apartments; the income range should be particularly broad. Orpheum Plaza Towers should meet the ratio of moderate-income units mandated by its subsidy.

South Bluffs
On a narrow strip of land between the railroad and the Bluffs, new, single-family, high-income town housing has been inserted. However, most housing in the South Bluffs will consist of loft apartments in vacated warehouse buildings. These conversions, to suit the lifestyles and tastes of young urban professionals, will increase as warehousing and light industry cease to be the economically highest and best use of the land.

New housing, which maintains the tissue of the area established by the warehousing, can contain smaller and more traditional types of apartment units. These would be primarily for couples and singles of middle and moderate income, employed downtown. A proportion of aided units in this housing type could help extend the income range from moderate to low-moderate, for the same population of downtown employees.

One Riverside Drive
This large project is both figuratively and literally down the road. When it is built, its mix of housing types should range from townhouses along the Bluffs to high-rise apartments near the Tennessee Brewery, related to the proposed commercial centre at the south end of South Main. Probably the majority of units will be garden apartments in the moderate- to middle-income range. Assisted units could serve low-moderate income workers and the elderly.

South Main
Although this is primarily a retail and office street, there should be apartments over some ground-floor uses, for occupants who want to live above the store.

It is important to the overall attractiveness of centre city that there be an arts presence on South Main – an area where real artists live, work and sell their wares. However, soon there will be no way for artists to afford property on South Main. Financing should be designed and made available now to help artists obtain a foothold in this area before values rise too steeply. Special efforts should be made to ensure that South Main is inviting to black artists as well as white.

East of South Main
Second and Third Streets as they run through this area will become important arterials delivering traffic downtown. Auto-oriented retail uses may be expected and should be encouraged here, as a means of keeping them out of the sensitive historic tissue of South Main and South Bluffs and the residential tissue of South Beale.

Within east South Main, it may be possible to consolidate parcels of land large enough to

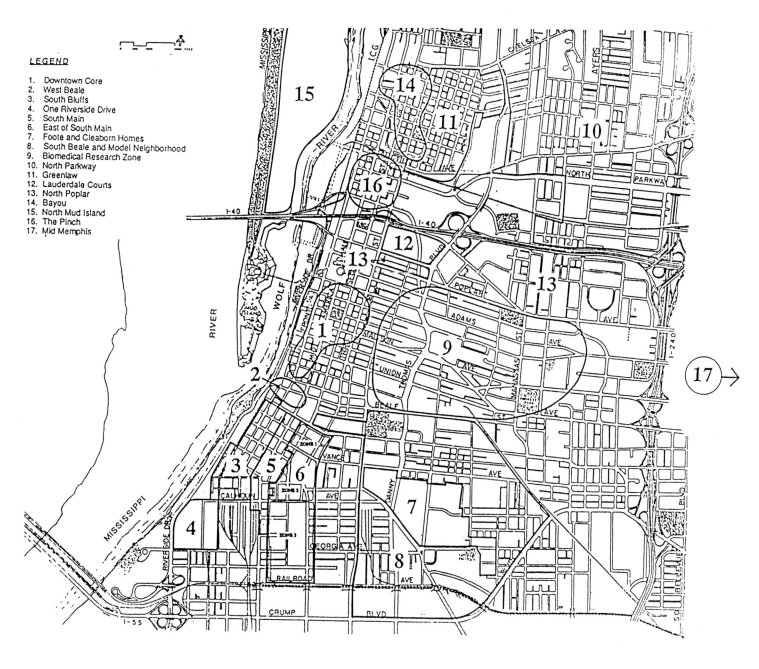

LEGEND

1. Downtown Core
2. West Beale
3. South Bluffs
4. One Riverside Drive
5. South Main
6. East of South Main
7. Foote and Cleaborn Homes
8. South Beale and Model Neighborhood
9. Biomedical Research Zone
10. North Parkway
11. Greenlaw
12. Lauderdale Courts
13. North Poplar
14. Bayou
15. North Mud Island
16. The Pinch
17. Mid Memphis

HOUSING STRATEGY AREAS

provide sites for new, low-moderate-income, assisted housing. This housing would be oriented toward the South Beale neighbourhood and would be suitable for families.

If a convenience retail centre were located at a mid-point on South Main, residents of east South Main could share shopping facilities with residents of areas to the west; this would help to link the communities. Another, more spiritual link would be through the uses in and around the Lorraine Motel.

Foote and Cleaborn Homes
The Center City Development Plan should sponsor rehabilitation at these homes as a major statement of faith. Steps toward the rehabilitation should figure in the first action plan, and planning for the rehabilitation should start now.

We recommend that the CCC sponsor The Tennessee Valley Center, as the planning team's consultant for minority issues, to meet with the Memphis Housing Authority to work out a plan for the rehabilitation of the project or portions of it.

What would this rehabilitation cover? Housing renewal? Re-landscaping? While we strongly back the Authority's resistance to sale of public housing units, changes in the direction of tenant control of procedures and admissions may well be in order. Is the Authority making or experimenting with changes of this nature? Is it experimenting with the allotting of communal open space to individual tenants for gardens? Are there other ideas for social as well as physical rehabilitation current with the Authority today that the CCC could support?

The South Beale Model Neighbourhood
This neighbourhood is the subject of a separate study. Here we discuss the centre city interest in the planning of an area that impinges on and is linked to the city centre.

South Beale is intended to become an area of primarily low-moderate-income housing that seams smoothly into the low-, moderate- and middle-income housing adjacent to it. Families should form a substantial portion of the residents and there should be the full range of community facilities needed for family living. Yet, Beale Street at the northern edge of this community should subtly pervade its experience and render it truly a centre city community.

Working opportunities for residents of South Beale should exist in centre city, the BRZ, the Medical Centre, St Jude's, and industrial areas to the south. The community is strategically located for work opportunities in all these areas.

Housing types should range from existing rehabilitated single-family housing to new townhouses and garden apartments. There is the possibility of high-rise apartment housing, probably for the elderly, associated with open space in or adjacent to the area. Most housing units in South Beale should be assisted in some way.

The CCC should encourage the initiation of rehabilitation at South Beale's northern edge, along Vance and Pontotoc, in order to create a climate suitable for residential development along Beale and Linden.

We originally recommended that the large, cleared site just south of Beale Street, between Second, Fourth, Lee and Linden, be considered as a 'land resource', to be used for an important regional or city-wide community facility that would help support Beale Street in particular and centre city in general. We felt the block's great strategic value (enhanced by the fact that it was owned by the city) justified maintaining it for such a purpose. However, the sports arena debate has demonstrated there is little likelihood a facility with the performance criteria needed would be located on this site. Meanwhile, UDAG funding has been obtained for Peabody Place and there seem to be prospects for early rehabilitation of South Main and South Bluffs, as well as for some high-rise housing at or near the west end of Beale. These projects, if built, could vastly increase the market for retail and cultural uses on Beale Street, without drawing arena crowds through the streets of South Beale. Nevertheless, the mandate would still exist to use the South Beale site for an important purpose that would help to achieve Center City goals.

In this context, a planned unit development for moderate-income housing could be the most strategic use for the site. It could initiate a programme for increasing moderate-income housing in the centre city and the BRZ and, owing to its visible location, could be an able demonstration of the value of such housing in centre city. This seems a suitable use for a strategically placed land resource.

The architecture of this housing should be urbane. Unlike most South Beale housing, which is almost suburban in character, this should be street-oriented, formal town housing that subtly relates to the architecture of Beale Street.

Biomedical Research Zone

In the broad plain between downtown and the Medical Centre, medically-related uses expanding from the Medical Centre should meet downtown-related uses spreading eastwards, to create an office park environment of relatively low buildings with space around them for parking. In this setting, sites should be assembled for the construction of garden apartments for middle- and moderate-income residents who work in both centres. This housing could serve workers who cannot afford the prices on the Bluffs or North Mud Island. It should be built before downtown development generates property values that make it impossible.

Housing sites should be sought in an area bounded by Fourth and Manassas, I-40 and Vance. Between Union, Thomas, Manassas and Jefferson, there may be sections where the closing of a street could produce an enclave suitable for planned unit development. Inward-looking, protective, residential environments might be attractive and reassuring to prospective residents who fear crime in the BRZ.

Victorian Village and Edison, Morris, and Forest Parks are amenities in this area, and may provide options for an occasional high-rise apartment building alongside a park. New developments would be more attractive if they were anchored by older houses. The restoration of old houses should be encouraged where possible.

Housing in the BRZ could extend south from residential areas north of Poplar Avenue; it would seam through BRZ work places, running at right angles to the east-west workstream and joining the residential uses south of Beale Street. Although interspersed with other uses, there should be enough housing to help combat the fear of crime. A convenience centre to serve the BRZ and North Poplar could be located on Poplar, near Danny Thomas, at the breakpoint between downtown and the Medical Centre.

Greenlaw

This area of historic, potentially beautiful houses set in yards with trees should be targeted to low-moderate-, moderate- and middle-income families with children. It could be an area of choice for the families of service workers, medical students and interns associated with St Jude's. It should feel like a self-contained community with strong community facilities within and adjoining it.

The CCC should encourage the initiation of renewal in Greenlaw near its western and southern edges, to support the recommendations for the Bayou and Pinch areas.

North Parkway

This is part of the horseshoe of housing that surrounds the work places of centre city and the Medical Centre. It probably orients primarily towards the Medical Centre but is also one in a series of housing options for the variegated work force of the expanding St Jude's.

Its treed, residential environment is an asset worth conserving against inroads from expressway-related uses.

Lauderdale Courts

This should be the second public housing target area sponsored by the CCC. It is well designed in terms of scale, density, and relationship between buildings, open space and landscape.

The same recommendations hold as for Foote and Cleaborn Homes to the south; however, because this project is part of the Elvis Presley story, there could possibly be further sponsorship available to it. How many

more world successes can we help to emerge from public housing in Memphis?

North Poplar

The same recommendations hold as for North Parkway. The block-wide strip on the north side of Poplar Avenue, between Third Street and Danny Thomas Boulevard, could be a site for new, assisted, moderate- and low-moderate-income housing.

Bayou

If the Bayou were rehabilitated, the area between the river and Greenlaw could be developed as a new, Bayou-related housing neighbourhood, different in character and denser than Greenlaw, targeted to a market that lies between the primarily moderate and lower-moderate-income housing in Greenlaw and the primarily middle and upper-income housing on North Mud Island.

When Front, Second and Third Streets become main arterials, Bayou, given its location and accessibility, could become a sought-after apartment area. Access across the railroad at Saffarans or Keel would increase the attractiveness of Bayou by relating it to recreation uses on the Wolf River. Local retail, serving Bayou and Greenlaw, could occur between Second and Third.

North Mud Island

Mud Island is a sand bar that formed between downtown Memphis and the Mississippi in the early years of this century. About four miles long and three-quarters of a mile wide at its widest, it defines the estuary and western bank of the Wolf River. The land configuration achieved its present shape when a levee was built at the northern end of the island to control the flooding of the Wolf River. At its southern tip, the Mud Island Entertainment Center has been built, but north of the I-40, Mud Island is virtually undeveloped. A park lines its western perimeter defining its edge along the river. A frontage road demarcates the park from privately owned land to the east.

During the last decade, several visions have been proposed for North Mud Island. One was of a new commercial and office area, where high-rise towers formed a bony spine down the centre of the island. A second vision contained a 'parkway', scaled to expressway dimensions, which travelled the length of the island and rose high above it at the southern end, to join the I-40 and cross the Wolf River estuary. This vision was devoted primarily to solving transportation problems on the mainland. A third vision projected a seven-storey townhousing crescent looking across the Wolf River. Post-Modern in its styling, this large-scaled wall of housing was reminiscent of grand-scale English or European city houses, perhaps of embankment housing on the Thames. In this vision a series of 12-storey tower buildings lined the Mississippi river edge, and on-lot parking, to accommodate the cars generated by the housing, was located in a band behind the housing, facing the Wolf River.

Trends in the 1980s made us question some assumptions of the earlier visions:

A high-rise office and commercial centre on the island would compete with the already ailing office economy downtown. As serious, the information on seismic problems along the Mississippi coastline in and near Memphis raised the question of the safety of constructing high-rise buildings on North Mud Island.

The plans for the FAP-3 'parkway' seemed to put an expensive facility in a location where the accessibility it provided could be least used. The size and location of the facility would leave little room on either side for development, and the limited access provided to the island itself would constrain development opportunities considerably. The placement of the highway would remove the opportunity to establish a convincing neighbourhood identity for housing on the island. More than this, the existence of FAP-3 appeared to predetermine that there would be a multi-level expressway between downtown and the Mississippi, further south.

The plan for embankment housing and towers offered quantities of two housing types that were already adequately served on the mainland, and lost the opportunity to build other housing types that would be popular, saleable, and also useful to broader centre city development aims. The vast parking lot proposed behind the housing seemed too great a price to pay to allow half the population to see the river.

As our study proceeded, it became apparent that much more housing was needed in Center City than now exists. Also certain segments of the housing market were not, and could not be, provided for on the mainland, owing to lack of space. In essence, if downtown was to compete with suburban East Memphis, it needed, within walking distance, a stock of housing similar to that in East Memphis, and this housing needed its own, attractive, neighbourhood identity, to establish its presence and suggest it as a possibility to people whose preferences would turn, first, towards the suburbs.

North Mud Island should be downtown's answer to Germantown. It should be a residential neighbourhood that is not exactly suburban but is desirable to some (though not all) people who would like to live in Germantown. It should be well linked to downtown for retail, entertainment and workplace services, and should offer housing options to business executives and managers whose location decisions affect the work opportunities of others in centre city.

Although North Mud Island should provide housing primarily at the upper third of the income scale, a range of incomes should be accommodated from low-moderate to high. Financial mechanisms should be evolved to ensure the representation of low-moderate-income residents within the area.

Owing to seismic problems, high-rise housing

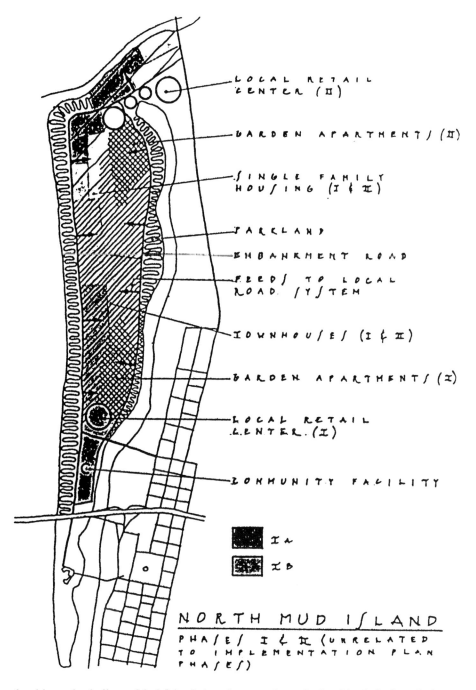

LOCAL RETAIL CENTER (II)

GARDEN APARTMENTS (II)

SINGLE FAMILY HOUSING (I & II)

PARKLAND

EMBANKMENT ROAD

FEEDS TO LOCAL ROAD SYSTEM

TOWNHOUSES (I & II)

GARDEN APARTMENTS (I)

LOCAL RETAIL CENTER (I)

COMMUNITY FACILITY

I A

I B

NORTH MUD ISLAND

PHASES I & II (UNRELATED TO IMPLEMENTATION PLAN PHASES)

should not be built on Mud Island, but the housing should include garden apartments, townhouses, semi-detached and detached houses. At a gross density of about nine units per acre, the island could house about 3,500 units; net residential densities would be considerably higher.

Although the plan should accommodate primarily the garden apartments and townhouses recommended by the market study, some units of high-income, single-family housing should be planned at the northern extremity of the island in relation to water. This housing will help attract the families of executives and managers; it will also help to produce the required image of a suburb in a city.

We have sketched a vision of a 'green country town' or 'garden city' for North Mud Island. Although most units will be attached and for rent, all should convey the image of a

garden suburb with pitched roofs, lawns and trees. There should be a strong presence of water. Parking for private automobiles should be available in *small*, landscaped courts, immediately adjacent to houses. 'A quiet place in the country is closer than you think,' should be the slogan for North Mud Island, as it is for Kimbrough Park in Germantown.

The suburban image is not one that architects and urban designers usually favour. Urbane, grand-scaled townhouses, based on the London terraces of John Nash or the Adam brothers, would be easy to propose here. However, people who like such housing are a small, rich minority, for whom only a few units should be built. Many who fall into this category will, in any case, want to live on Cotton Row or in the converted offices and warehouses of downtown and the South Bluffs.

There is no one 'correct' way of living in

the city, and centre city will fare better if it can offer a variety of housing types. Among the types the plan proposes, the 'garden city' housing on Mud Island is crucial to the objective of competing with other housing in the region.

Uses other than residential on North Mud Island should be limited to those that are related to residences, for example, convenience retail, medical offices, and park land. The only commercial uses should be two small convenience-retail centres, one to the north at the Levee Road and the other at the Auction Avenue bridge.

Two-worker families with small children might form an important market segment for housing on Mud Island. For them, child care would be a major concern and an elementary school would be a *sine qua non*. This school should be located on the mainland, where it can be shared by families east of the Wolf River and by those who work downtown and want their children in school near their work place. Families with middle- and high-school children would probably be prepared to have them travel to schools within the region.

Vacant land south of Auction Avenue should serve initially as a picnic ground for the Mud Island Entertainment Center, but should be reserved for a public or community facility, connected with the Center.

The road network that serves the island must be a *local* network. The garden city environment would be vitiated by an arterial 'parkway' down the centre of Mud Island, although a local embankment road along the Wolf River would be desirable. It should provide access to residential subdivision roads to the west and to public parkland to the east, on the Wolf River.

For those living in the southern reaches of

THE DESIRED IMAGE

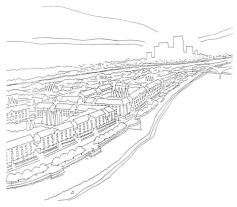

THE UNDESIRED IMAGE

the island, a walk to work would be a distinct possibility. Rubber-tyred transit should be available for others.

A CCC plan for North Mud Island is needed now, in order to produce guidelines for the private sector, before development is imminent and before plans are devised that go against centre city interests. However, the market study warns that the actual development of Mud Island should not be rushed; if it

is, Mud Island housing will compete with mainland housing that, in the short run, will be more necessary to the achievement of the success of downtown.

Nevertheless, a few single-family detached units could be built at once at the northern end of the island, facing the Mississippi. These would appeal to urban 'frontiers people', who liked the original South Bluffs townhouses but want a detached home on a large lot. The next priority would be moderate-income garden apartments in enclaves near Auction Avenue, on the Wolf River side of the island. These should be accompanied by limited numbers of middle- and upper-middle-income townhousing overlooking the Mississippi (for some of this housing the Thames embankment image could possibly apply). When there is a critical mass of housing, the Auction Avenue retail centre should be developed to serve the southern end of the island.

Because initial increments will consist largely of moderate-income housing for singles and young marrieds, they will not require the child care and education facilities that will determine the success of the community in subsequent phases.

The Pinch
With development all around them, the intimately scaled retail and community uses on North Main street in the Pinch could be revived to support a district of unusual character. Paralleling development patterns in South Main and the South Bluffs, there is here the possibility of loft apartments and living-above-the-store. Between North Main Street and the Wolf River around Front Street, there are good locations for high-rise apartment buildings with views across the Mississippi – although this depends on whether

A GARDEN CITY ON NORTH MUD ISLAND

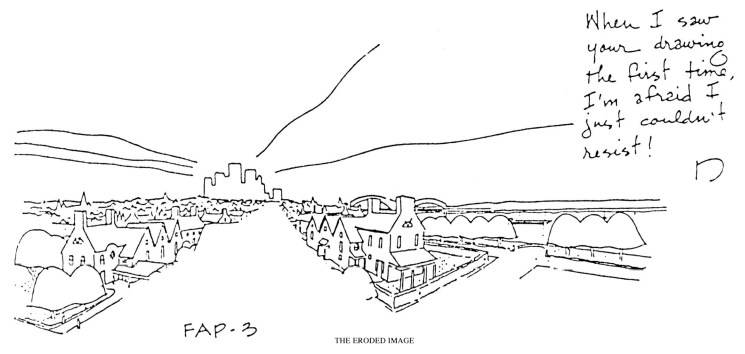

FAP·3

When I saw your drawing the first time, I'm afraid I just couldn't resist!

THE ERODED IMAGE

seismic risks can be mitigated and on whether the arena is located at the southern end of this area.

Midtown

The housing stock of midtown Memphis is an important resource for centre city. Much appreciated by Memphians, its well built single-family houses on tree-lined residential streets and its gracious, brick apartments, set around treed courts, have in them people who would not be happy in modern apartments or townhouses. Were this stock unavailable, most midtown residents would probably move to East Memphis. A few could be candidates for loft apartments in the South Bluffs, but most probably require the traditional apartment plans available in midtown rather than the informality offered by converted warehousing.

Many people from midtown work in the Medical Centre and downtown; if the Local Distributor transportation plan, the Peabody Place project, and the augmentation of Beale Street were implemented, we believe there would be a much greater use of downtown by midtown residents, for work, shopping, and entertainment. The original linkages between downtown and its streetcar suburb would be re-established. However, if these downtown opportunities are not provided, and if inroads are made on the residential integrity of mid-

town through expansion there of institutional facilities or demolition for parking, a balance could be tipped, the midtown neighbourhood could dissipate, and its residents move to East Memphis. With them would go a series of small but important cultural facilities that have grown up in conjunction with this special community and that have linkages with downtown.

Midtown is therefore in a swing situation; depending on what is done, it could head west or east. The removal of midtown support, and potential support, from downtown would be a severe blow to the aims and prospects of renewal for Center City. The maintenance of this interesting housing stock is therefore a prime necessity for centre city. Its rehabilitation and intelligent intensification would be a benefit, particularly as midtown itself lacks work locations.

A plan should be made for midtown supporting its residential character and limiting the inroads of non-residential uses by redirecting Medical Centre expansion toward the BRZ.

CONCLUSION

The housing strategies outlined are multidimensional and complex but no more so than is needed to attain the aims of the Center City Development Plan. Support for a vital down-

town will come from the many types of housing and the many housing markets that can exist around the centre city.

While the strategies for middle- and upper-income residential development place emphasis on environmental amenities and their maintenance as support services to stimulate private investment, the housing strategies for low- and moderate-income residents call for more direct action and a far greater commitment of public resources. But the benefits are expected to outweigh the costs, partly because they include the environmental improvements needed to attract residents, visitors, retailers, corporations, and investors downtown.

If low- and moderate-income residential development does not figure in the formula for centre city revitalisation, Memphis risks being left with an anaemic downtown. In the absence of a dynamic centre, achievement of the metropolitan economic development agenda seems unlikely

Notes

1 Barbara Radice, *Memphis: Research, Experiences, Results, Failures and Successes of New Design*, Editoriale Electa, Milan; Rizzoli International, New York, 1984, p 26.
2 Conducted in 1985 by subconsultant Arthur D Little Inc, Cambridge, Mass.

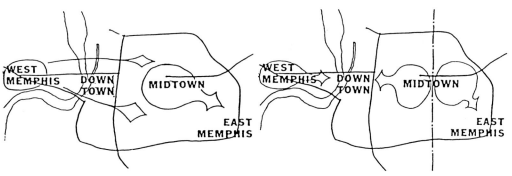

WILL MIDTOWN TURN EAST OR WEST?

ABOVE AND BELOW: SIDE VIEWS OF HOUSE

HOUSE ON LONG ISLAND V, 1985-90
EASTERN LONG ISLAND, NEW YORK

This is a summer house for a family of four. Set within beautiful woods, the house recalls Shingle Style architecture of the area, in its generous scale, ample porch, double-hung sash and abundance of cedar shingles. Because no view is dominant in this location, the house is like a pavilion without distinctions between back and front or particular accommodation for a front entrance. Its sloping roof predominates and, with the large

window on the east side, creates a big scale in contrast with the variety of smaller elements – windows, doors, porch, etc – around the base of the house.

The ground-floor interior spaces look into the woods. Downstairs, space flows around a central fireplace and stairway and up into the floors above. The bedrooms are attic-like; the second-floor children's bedrooms contain built-in furniture, like cabins in a boat.

ABOVE: MODEL; *BELOW*: NORTH AND SOUTH ELEVATIONS

131

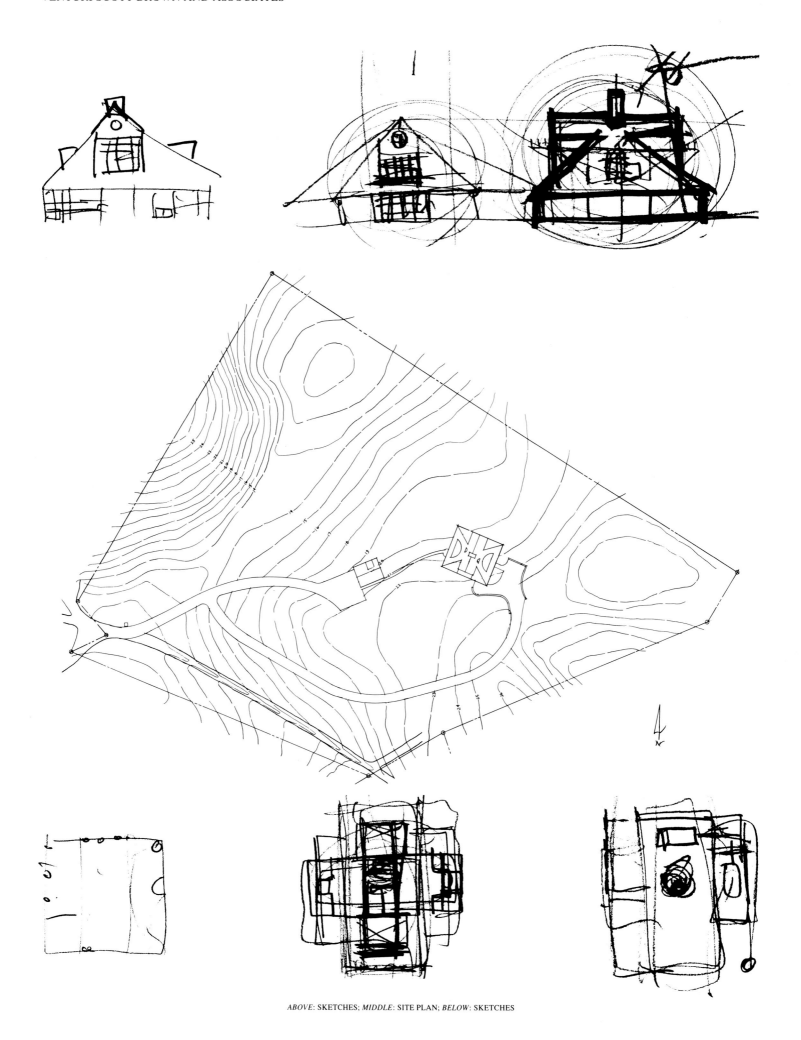

ABOVE: SKETCHES; *MIDDLE*: SITE PLAN; *BELOW*: SKETCHES

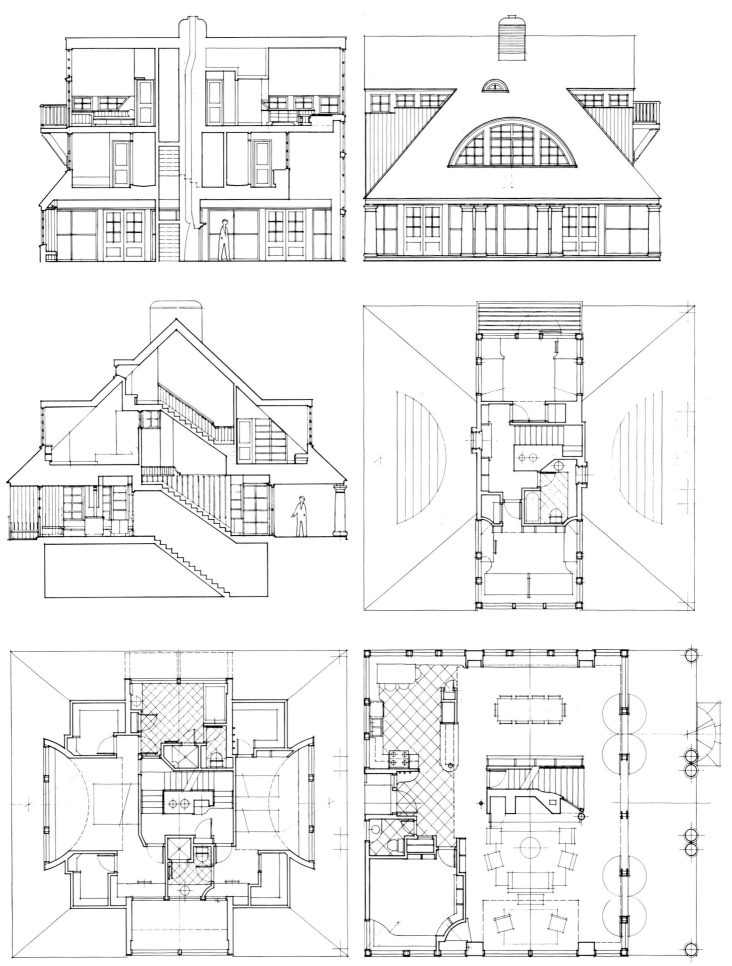

ABOVE: LONG SECTION AND WEST ELEVATION; *MIDDLE*: CROSS SECTION AND SECOND-FLOOR PLAN; *BELOW*: FIRST AND GROUND-FLOOR PLANS

HOUSE IN MAINE, 1986
MAINE

This 5,000-square-foot vacation house is built on a wooded coastal site that affords dramatic views of the ocean. Its design is reminiscent of Shingle Style cottages in the area. On the exterior, natural-finish cedar, local fieldstone and dark green trim help to harmonise house and landscape.

Inside, the house accommodates a family of four and numerous guests. Although the emphasis is on casual living outdoors, custom work in wood and local stone impart an air of elegance.

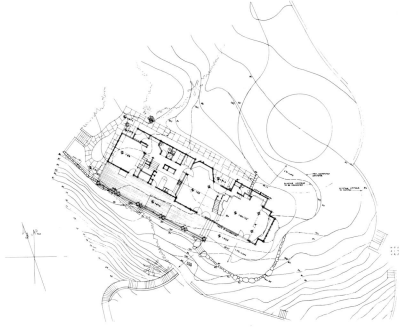

OPPOSITE: LONG VIEW OF HOUSE; *ABOVE*: VIEW OF EAST ELEVATION AND VIEW OF HALL; *BELOW*: SITE PLAN

ABOVE: VIEW OF NORTH ELEVATION; *BELOW*: VIEW OF VERANDAH

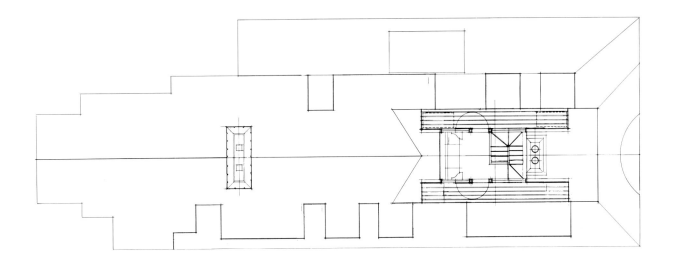

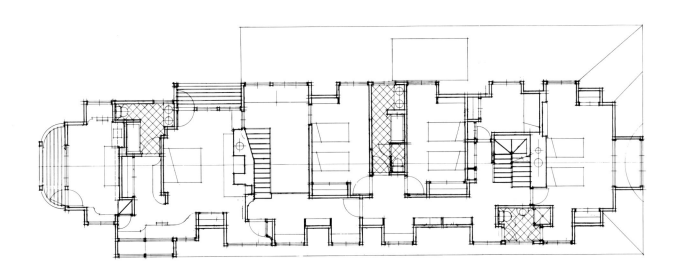

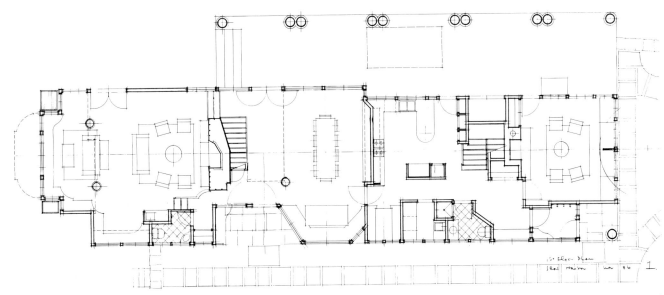

FROM ABOVE: ROOF PLAN; FIRST-FLOOR PLAN; GROUND-FLOOR PLAN

ABOVE: VIEW OF SOUTH ELEVATION; *BELOW*: VIEW OF LIVING-ROOM

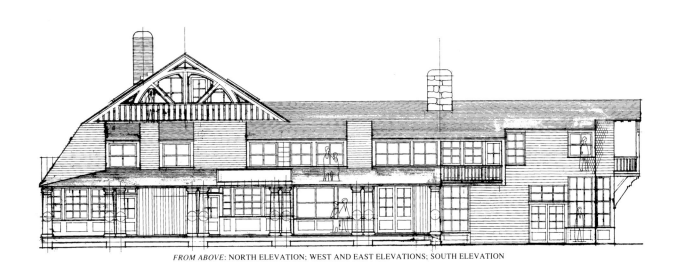

FROM ABOVE: NORTH ELEVATION; WEST AND EAST ELEVATIONS; SOUTH ELEVATION

HOUSE IN TUXEDO PARK, PROJECT, 1987 TO PRESENT
NEW YORK

A weekend and summer house in, and we think at home in, Tuxedo Park, Pierre Lorillard's planned Romantic suburb, where Bruce Price created inspiring examples of domestic Shingle Style architecture in the 1880s. The building combines asymmetrical wings and a turret, in the late-Richardsonian, picturesque manner; but these elements are suggested, vestigial or embryonic and, in combination, they create an uneasy whole.

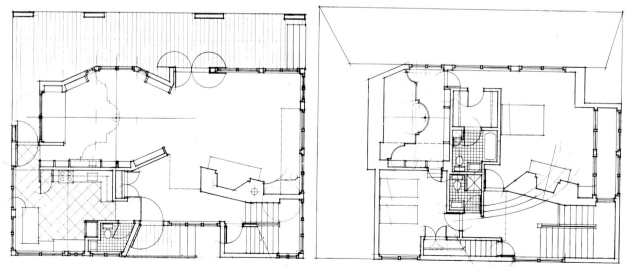

ABOVE: NORTH AND EAST ELEVATIONS; *MIDDLE*: SECTION LOOKING NORTH AND SOUTH ELEVATION; *BELOW*: GROUND AND FIRST-FLOOR PLANS

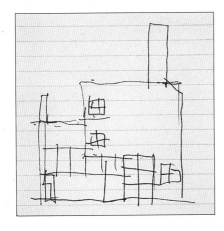 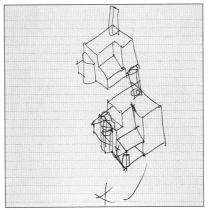 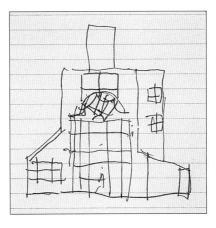

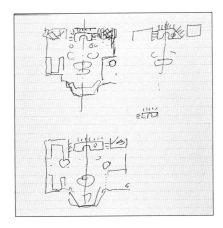  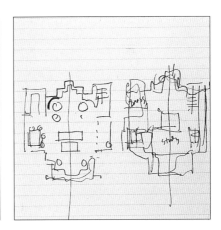

SKETCHES FOR A HOUSE, 1990

These notations by Robert Venturi set down his initial thoughts on a small house with big scale; a 'dream' house for a narrow site near a city. The drawings trace the genesis and early development of a design.

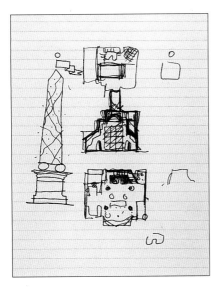  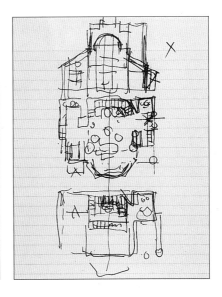

CHRONOLOGY OF HOUSES AND HOUSING PROJECTS

ROBERT VENTURI

1957
Pearson House, Project
Chestnut Hill, Philadelphia

ROBERT VENTURI, COPE AND LIPPINCOTT ASSOCIATED ARCHITECTS

1958
James B Duke House, Renovation
Institute of Fine Arts, New York University
New York, New York

1959
Williams House, Renovation
Philadelphia, Pennsylvania

Foulkeways, Gwynnedd, Project
Gwynnedd, Pennsylvania

Altschul House, Renovation
New York University
New York, New York

Beach House, Project
East Coast, United States of America

VENTURI AND SHORT

1960
Mills House Extension
Princeton, New Jersey

1961
Miller House, Project
Easthampton, New York

Guild House
Philadelphia, Pennsylvania
Associated Architect: Cope and Lippincott

Vanna Venturi House
Chestnut Hill, Pennsylvania

1962
Meiss House, Project
Princeton, New Jersey

VENTURI AND RAUCH

1965
Haas Greenhouse
Ambler, Pennsylvania

Frug Houses I and II, Project
Princeton, New Jersey

1967
Lieb House
Loveladies, New Jersey

Brighton Beach Housing Competition
Brighton Beach, New York

1968
Hersey House, Project
Hyannisport, Massachusetts

D'Agostino House, Project
Clinton, New York

South Street, Planning Study. Housing
Strategy
Philadelphia, Pennsylvania

Wike House, Project
Devon, Pennsylvania

1969
Washington Square West Housing, Project
Philadelphia, Pennsylvania

1970
California City Planning Study
California City, California

Trubek and Wislocki Houses
Nantucket, Massachusetts

House in Connecticut
Greenwich, Connecticut

'Remedial Housing for Architects
or Learning from Levittown'
Research Projects, Yale University
New Haven, Connecticut

1972
Venturi House, Wissahickon Avenue
Philadelphia, Pennsylvania

Wissahickon Avenue Housing, Project
Philadelphia, Pennsylvania

Addition to House in Sea Isle City
Sea Isle City, New Jersey

Fairmount Manor
Community Housing Plan
Philadelphia, Pennsylvania

South Central Philadelphia, Plan

Philadelphia, Pennsylvania

Lieb House, Renovation
Penn Valley, Pennsylvania

1973
Haas Carriage Shed
Ambler, Pennsylvania

Lieb Pool House, Project
Penn Valley, Pennsylvania

1974
Tucker House
Westchester County, New York

Dream House, Project
Jersey Shore, Pennsylvania

Home Section of 'Signs of Life: Symbols
in the American City', Exhibition,
Smithsonian Institution, Washington,
District of Columbia

Carefree Phoenix Land Development Study
Phoenix, Arizona

1975
House in Vail
Vail, Colorado

House in Bermuda
Tuckers Town, Bermuda

Vanna Venturi Addition, Project
Chestnut Hill, Pennsylvania

1976
House in Connecticut Addition, Project
Greenwich, Connecticut

1977
Haas House, Interior Renovation
Ambler, Pennsylvania

Old City, Planning Study
Housing Recommendations
Philadelphia, Pennsylvania

House on Long Island I, Project
Long Island, New York

Eclectic House, Project

House in Absecon, Project
Absecon, New Jersey

1978
House in Delaware
New Castle County, Delaware

Brant House Extension II, Project
Greenwich, Connecticut

Princeton Housing, Project
Princeton, New Jersey

Land Development Study
Princeton Township, New Jersey

1979
House
Pittsburgh, Pennsylvania

Chinatown Housing
Philadelphia, Pennsylvania

Coxe-Hayden House and Studio
Block Island, Rhode Island

'Mount Vernon' House, Project

**VENTURI, RAUCH AND
SCOTT BROWN**

1980
Metropolitan Tower Apartments
Philadelphia, Pennsylvania

Rockefeller and Mathey Colleges,
Renovation
Princeton University
Princeton, New Jersey

1981
Blair and Little Halls, Renovations
Princeton University
Princeton, New Jersey

House on Long Island II, Project
Long Island, New York

Khulafa Street Mixed Use Building
with Housing, Project
Baghdad, Iraq

House on Nantucket Island
Nantucket Island, Massachusetts

1982
House on Long Island III
Long Island, New York

1983
Republic Square District Master Plan and
Museum Location Study
Housing prototypes
Austin, Texas

Winterthur Housing, Project
Wilmington, Delaware

House on Long Island IV
Glen Cove, New York

1984
Library for a House in Northern Italy
Lake Orta, Italy

Forbes College, Renovation
Princeton University
Princeton, New Jersey

Center City, Development Plan
Housing Strategy
Memphis, Tennessee

Faculty Housing, Project
Institute for Advanced Studies
Princeton, New Jersey

1985
Sunshine Dream Village, Project
Orlando, Florida

Pearl Houses
Palm Beach West, Florida

House on Long Island V
Eastern Long Island, New York

East Campus Residential College Study
Duke University, Durham, North Carolina

1986
Fan Pier Apartment Building, Project
Boston, Massachusetts
Master Plan Architect: Cesar Pelli

House in Maine
Maine

1987
House in Tuxedo Park
New York, New York

**VENTURI SCOTT BROWN AND
ASSOCIATES**

1990
Sketches for a House

Prototype Houses, Project
Mitsui, Tokyo, Japan

1991
House (Currently in design)
Nantucket, Massachusetts

ATTRIBUTIONS

Guild House: *Robert Venturi and Gerod Clark with Frank Kawasaki. Associate Firm: Cope and Lipincott, Architects.*

Vanna Venturi House: *Robert Venturi with Arthur Jones.*

Meiss House, Project: *Robert Venturi and William Short.*

Lieb House: *Robert Venturi and John Rauch with Gerod Clark.*

Brighton Beach Housing Competition: *Robert Venturi and John Rauch with Gerod Clark, Denise Scott Brown, and associated with Frank Kawasaki.*

D'Agostino House, Project: *Robert Venturi and John Rauch with WG Clark.*

Wike House: *Robert Venturi.*

Trubek and Wislocki Houses: *Robert Venturi and John Rauch with Terry Vaughan. Associate Firm: Chris Holland.*

House in Connecticut: *Robert Venturi and John Rauch with Gerod Clark, Arthur Jones, Denise Scott Brown, WG Clark, James Greifendorf, Paul Hirshorn, Terry Vaughan and Anthony Pellecchia.*

Addition to House in Connecticut, Project: *Robert Venturi with Missy Maxwell.*

Signs of Life: Symbols in the American City, Exhibition. *Organised by Denise Scott Brown, Steven Izenour and Robert Venturi with Janet Colesberry, Missy Maxwell, Paul Hirshorn, Stephen Kieran, Daniel Rauch, Dan Scully, Douglas Southworth and James H Timberlake.*

Wissahickon Avenue Housing, Project: *Robert Venturi.*

Tucker House: *Robert Venturi and John Rauch with Douglas Southworth.*

House in Bermuda: *Robert Venturi and John Rauch with John Chase. Associate Firm: Onions, Bouchard & McCulloch.*

House in Vail: *Robert Venturi with Robert Renfro, Douglas Southworth and Elizabeth Plater-Zyberk. Associate Firm: William J Ruoff.*

Eclectic House, Project: *Robert Venturi.*

Princeton Housing, Project: *Robert Venturi and John Rauch with James H Timberlake, Steven Izenour and James Allen Schmidt.*

House in Delaware: *Robert Venturi and John Chase with Janet Colesberry, Ronald McCoy, Paul Muller and Frederic Schwartz.*

Chinatown Housing: *Robert Venturi and John Rauch with Arthur Jones, James Bradberry, David Brisbin, Robert DeSilets, David Marohn and Christopher Smith.*

Coxe-Hayden House: *Robert Venturi and John Rauch with Frederic Schwartz.*

House on Nantucket Island: *Robert Venturi with James Bradberry and Roc Caivano.*

House on Long Island III, Project: *Robert Venturi with James H Timberlake, Steven Izenour, David Marohn, Christine Matheu, C Stanley Runyan, Jeffrey D Ryan and Maurice Weintraub. Associate Firm: Clayton Morey.*

Winterthur Housing, Project: *Robert Venturi with Steven Izenour and David Schaaf.*

House on Long Island IV: *Robert Venturi with Frederic Schwartz and Perry Kulper.*

Plan for the Republic Square District, Austin: *Denise Scott Brown with Vincent Hauser, Robert Venturi and Miles Ritter. Associate Firm: Halcyon Inc.*

House at Stony Creek: *Steven Izenour with Christine Matheu.*

Library for a House in Northern Italy: *Robert Venturi with James Bradberry and Maurice Weintraub.*

Sunshine Dream Village, Project: *Robert Venturi with Roc Caivano and Maurice Weintraub.*

Pearl Houses: *Robert Venturi with Perry Kulper and Willis Pember.*

Memphis Center City Development Plan: *Denise Scott Brown with Gabrielle London and David Schaaf. Consultants: KKFS, AD Little Inc, Urban Partners, Williamson/ Awsumb, Tennessee Valley Center, Robert L Morris.*

House on Long Island V: *Robert Venturi with Perry Kulper and Fran Read. Consultants: Keast and Hood (structural) and Fred Weber, PE (mechanical).*

House in Maine: *Robert Venturi with Roc Caivano, Gabrielle London and Maurice Weintraub.*

House in Tuxedo Park: *Robert Venturi with Dan McCoubrey and Steve Wiesenthal. Consultants: Keast and Hood (structural) and Basil Green (mechanical).*

PHOTO CREDITS

Guild House: *Frank Kawasaki, Steven Izenour, Mark Cohn and George Pohl.*
Vanna Venturi House: *Rollin La France and George Pohl.*
Lieb House: *Stephen Hill.*
Brighton Beach Housing Competition: *Stephen Hill.*
House in Connecticut: *Cervin Robinson.*
Signs of Life: Symbols in the American City: *Steven Shore.*
Trubek and Wislocki Houses: *Steven Izenour.*
Tucker House: *Tom Crane and Tom Bernard.*
House in Delaware: *Tom Bernard and Matt Wargo.*
Chinatown Housing: *Tom Bernard.*
House in Bermuda: *Tom Bernard.*
House in Vail: *Steven Izenour.*
Coxe-Hayden House: *Tom Bernard and Tom Crane.*
House on Long Island III: *Tom Bernard.*
House on Long Island IV: *Matt Wargo.*
House at Stony Creek: *Tom Bernard and Matt Wargo.*
Pearl Houses: *Matt Wargo.*
House on Long Island V: *Matt Wargo.*
House in Maine: *Matt Wargo.*